"Parents unknowingly destroy [. . .] *Digital Detox* exposes the har[. . .] giving hope and practical direction for parents."

Francis and Lisa Chan, *New York Times* bestselling authors

"I don't know a parent who isn't concerned about the amount of time their kids are spending on screens. For many moms and dads, screen time is their biggest trigger. After all, devices can become divisive—dividing us from one another, schoolwork, and even health and happiness. Unfortunately, we don't know what to do about it or where to start. Molly DeFrank paves the way. This brilliant book is a game changer for parents. It will transform the way families engage with their screens—and ultimately how they engage with each other. Molly is a wise, worthy, and witty guide. She will help families take charge of their devices—instead of letting devices take charge of families."

Wendy Speake, author of *The 40-Day Social Media Fast*
and co-author of *Triggers: Exchanging Parents' Angry
Reactions for Gentle Biblical Responses*

"*Digital Detox* is a personable, hands-on guide to making your kids' and even your own lives a whole lot better. One big surprise: Your kids are likely to thank you for taking action. Get this book!"

Richard Freed, PhD, author of *Wired Child*

"I recommend this book for all parents of young children. It's a fact-based, funny, practical guide for how to get kids off their screens and back into real life."

Anna Lembke, MD, *New York Times* bestselling author
of *Dopamine Nation: Finding Balance in the Age of Indulgence*

"In today's tech-driven world, *Digital Detox* is an essential resource for parents. With grace and humor, Molly DeFrank combines real-world examples with practical tips to give parents the tools and confidence they need to make lasting changes. Much more than a how-to guide, *Digital Detox* offers hope and inspiration to families seeking a more balanced relationship with technology."

Kristin Demery, author of *One Good Word a Day: 365 Invitations to Encourage, Deepen, and Refine Your Faith*

"Finally! A practical guide that shows us parents how to navigate raising our kids in a technology-driven world. As a fellow Christian mama, I love how Molly lays it all out there. Her advice is realistic and useful, and her stories are relatable and encouraging. It's time we reset our approach to digital entertainment in the home, and my husband and I agree—this book is the perfect first step for every parent to take!"

Heidi Anderson, author and Christian influencer, @thismotherhen

"*Digital Detox* is a well-researched, sophisticated guide to out-smarting the addictive pandemic of digital entertainment—the furtive electronic cocaine that is rapidly destroying the creative childhood and intellectual drive of too many American children. In part thanks to the other pandemic, screen time for many kids has reached a mind-blowing eight hours a day. In addition to her broad knowledge, Mrs. DeFrank translates her firsthand experience as a working mom and foster mom into thoughtful, practical advice. If you are a parent, this book will change your life. And more importantly, the life of your kids. Believe me, they will thank you."

Peter C. Whybrow, MD, author of *The Well-Tuned Brain: The Remedy for a Manic Society*

"Molly DeFrank's important book is a useful resource for parents concerned about the effects of tech overuse on their children. Her honest insights on parenting, along with her practical action steps, are much-needed tools we can use to protect our kids."

Joe Clement, teacher and co-author of *Screen Schooled*

"Molly has managed to overcome what has become all too common in households all over—battles with our children about screen time. With practical advice and tons of conviction, *Digital Detox* is a great resource for parents of all ages."

Matt Miles, teacher and co-author of *Screen Schooled*

"Molly DeFrank has written a must-read primer for anyone who is ready to reset their family's digital world! Her easy-to-follow two-week plan will support you from beginning to end of your detox. This book is an incredible, thoughtful, and unique way we can all benefit from minimizing technology within our families."

Monica Gomez, speech language pathologist

"'Doctor, is the time she spends on her phone bad for her eyes?'—a worthwhile question I am often asked. But the deeper and more important question relates to her human development rather than her visual development. Mrs. DeFrank has written an accessible and important handbook for parents looking for guidance in our technocentric culture."

Jeffrey C. Krohn, OD, FAAO

"Too many children are trading in wonder and adventure for hours of sitting still staring at a screen. We need more voices like Molly DeFrank's to pull us away from mind-numbing entertainment. Digital harms and addictions can no longer be ignored. It's time to rise up as parents. A digital detox in your home is doable! This book is incredibly practical and will help you transform your home for the better, one day at a time."

Arlene Pellicane, author of *Screen Kids*
and host of the *Happy Home* podcast

"If you've got a love-hate relationship with screens in your home, *Digital Detox* is the guidebook you've been looking for. With her signature honesty and spot-on hilarity, Molly shows us exactly how we can help our kids break free from the grip of tech and recapture the magic of childhood."

Kayse Pratt, founder of Anchored Women

DIGITAL
DETOX

DIGITAL
DETOX

THE TWO-WEEK TECH RESET FOR KIDS

Molly DeFrank

BETHANYHOUSE
a division of Baker Publishing Group
Minneapolis, Minnesota

© 2022 by Molly DeFrank

Published by Bethany House Publishers
11400 Hampshire Avenue South
Minneapolis, Minnesota 55438
www.bethanyhouse.com

Bethany House Publishers is a division of
Baker Publishing Group, Grand Rapids, Michigan

Printed in the United States of America

Library of Congress Cataloging-in-Publication Data
Names: DeFrank, Molly, author.
Title: Digital detox : the two-week tech reset for kids / Molly DeFrank.
Description: Minneapolis, Minnesota : Bethany House Publishers, a division of
    Baker Publishing Group, [2022]
Identifiers: LCCN 2021056247 | ISBN 9780764238765 (trade paper) | ISBN
    9780764240584 (casebound) | ISBN 9781493435753 (ebook)
Subjects: LCSH: Creative ability. | Detoxification (Health) | Human behavior. |
    Internet—Social aspects. | Technological innovations—Social aspects.
Classification: LCC BF408 .D4453 2022 | DDC 153.3/5—dc23/eng/20211216
LC record available at https://lccn.loc.gov/2021056247

Some names and details in this book have been changed to preserve privacy.

Cover design by Emily Weigel

Author represented by Books & Such Literary Management

Baker Publishing Group publications use paper produced from sustainable forestry practices and post-consumer waste whenever possible.

22 23 24 25 26 27 28   7 6 5 4 3 2 1

For Dad

Contents

Contents

Introduction

"MOM, THANK YOU so much for taking our screens away," my ten-year-old daughter said out of the blue, a few months after our digital detox.

I nearly spat out my LaCroix. *Seriously?* is what my brain said. My mouth had the wherewithal to say something else. "Sweetie, you're welcome. . . . Can I ask why you're thanking me?"

"I just . . . feel happier. I read so many more books, I play outside more, I play with my siblings more. Also, my eyes and head used to hurt after I played video games." My nine- and seven-year-old sons were standing nearby and nodded in agreement.

I couldn't believe my ears.

My Minecraft-loving, LEGO Star Wars–battling, tablet-tapping children were *thanking me* for depriving them of their formerly favorite hobbies? My husband and I had noticed behavioral and mood improvements in our kids immediately when we began our family's detox. But I wasn't expecting the kids to *thank us*. Especially considering that when we broke the news to them initially, they practically rent their garments.

But after the screen daze was removed, the kids enjoyed more positive interactions with each other; they weren't in fight-or-flight mode every day. They spent more time honing real-life skills like piano, drawing, writing, biking, football. With those skills came confidence, stoking their desires to further hone their talents. What started as a two-week screen break turned into a complete technology overhaul in our family with five kids under ten. The simple decision to unplug and reset changed our lives in the best way.

I initially chose two weeks arbitrarily. Mostly because I thought it was all I could handle without requiring five nannies, remembering that we cannot afford five nannies, and then settling for breathing into a paper bag. I assumed that cutting out screens would create an impossible amount of work for me, that I'd be thrust into the role of entertainment instructor, court jester, or camp counselor. Richard Simmons meets Jojo Siwa.

This turned out not to be the case. But I didn't know that on Screen Detox Eve. Two weeks turned out to be just enough time to see how kids behave without the technology haze that infects their sweet personalities. It was enough time to observe the refreshing benefits of detox mode and decide that we would continue it, with the kids' blessing, for months. With newfound clarity, we then created a long-term plan that allowed for the best parts of tech and cut out the parts that were morphing my darlings into swamp creatures.

Before we started our detox years ago, I'd read exactly zero books, guides, or studies on the topic. I don't advise taking this route—unless you enjoy off-roading while blindfolded. In other words, we've made tremendous discoveries and progress, mistakes and recoveries along the way. In the years since, I've asked and searched for the answers to every question: Why did the detox work so quickly? Why were screens causing a problem in the first place? I've read the studies and books and talked with doctors, teachers, parents, and therapists from across the spectrum. I've taken what we've learned and used it to coach several families through their own detoxes. Some friends, some strangers. One hundred percent of these families were thrilled with the results of their detox.

These are actual responses from real parents who have used my tips and guidance to digitally detox their kids:

> "My eight-year-old finished nine chapter books during our detox! My older boys have fallen in love with a new sport, basketball!"
>
> "Before our detox, our kids were always so focused on phones. They were on their minds constantly. Their first words when we saw them were usually 'Can I use your phone?' They would choose the phone over a beautiful day—but not after our detox."
>
> "Fighting is at an all-time low, no complaints about being bored, all my kids are reading more without me asking."
>
> "My mom watched them for the first time since the detox yesterday, and she could not believe the change."
>
> "There aren't enough words for how this has changed the entire climate of our home!"
>
> "My girls have stopped asking for their iPads and started doing other activities."
>
> "Because of the detox, we have so much more time to connect as a family."
>
> "This was so much easier than we thought it would be, and I can't believe how quickly we saw results."
>
> "Our kids' behavior was so much better during our detox that we kept going. A year later, we have made easy and permanent changes that have noticeably helped our kids."
>
> "Molly . . . I have different kids!"

The digital detox and the home environment created by its implementation have proven life-changing for honors students and high achievers as well as for children from trauma, drug-addicted teenagers, and your normal pizza-obsessed, video-game-loving nine-year-old. In short, the digital detox is for everyone living in today's tech-saturated world.[1]

What began as off-roading without a map ended when we stumbled into a promising and refreshing oasis. In the pages ahead, you will find tips, tricks, and a route for your own successful two-week digital detox and beyond. This book is the practical guide I wish I had when we started. The pages ahead will show you the way and help you navigate hazards, leading you to your ultimate destination: A home that no longer feels bogged down by too much screen time. A healthy relationship with the best that tech has to offer. A home where tech can be used to enhance real life, not supplant it.

The path forward: the detox

If you cared enough to pick up this book, I bet you are a loving parent, feeling the weight of digital entertainment overload. You've always been mindful to set limits, but you're still unsettled by bad moods or upsetting behaviors. You don't have a perfect handle on balancing your kids' technology.

You want your kids to enjoy but not gorge, to cultivate healthy habits with screens.

But you're nervous to take the leap toward anything drastic.

You have big-picture ideals for your kids' tech use, but aren't sure how to get from the status quo to your end goal.

You are not alone.

The path from the status quo to a tech-healthy home doesn't cost a cent. It is simple, and easier than you can possibly imagine. The fighting, grumpiness, and out-of-control behavior can be reversed, almost immediately, through a simple detox combined with some good old-fashioned parental redirection.

That path forward is in the pages ahead. And as Dad and Mom, there's no one on the planet better suited to guide your kids.

How to use this book

I recommend you read the first half of the book (through part 1, "UNDO the Tech Trance," which outlines the steps of the detox) before starting your detox. You will also want to refer back to it throughout your fourteen-day detox. All you'll need is this book, a basic notebook or journal, and parental resolve. The first two you can find on Amazon. And the third in the bottom of a strong cup of coffee.

I recommend you read the second half of the book (part 2, "Now What? Sustaining Your Results") toward the end of your detox. This section will help you create a long-term plan that reincorporates just the right amount of digital entertainment for your family.

If you are an overachiever, you can read the entire thing before starting. But I don't recommend beginning your detox before finishing the first half of the book.

Ready? Let's go!

1

Parenting Challenges for a New Generation—The Problem

I wake up in cold sweats every so often thinking, what did we bring to the world? . . . Did we really bring a nuclear bomb with information that can . . . blow up people's brains and reprogram them?

TONY FADELL, SENIOR VICE PRESIDENT, APPLE

Wo didn't sign up for the digital lives we now lead. They were instead, to a large extent, crafted in boardrooms to serve the interests of a select group of technology investors.

CAL NEWPORT, *DIGITAL MINIMALISM*

MY FIVE KIDS were home with the babysitter. I don't remember my exact errands that day, but as a stay-at-home mom of many, it didn't matter. I would've welcomed the relative calm of a root canal appointment as if it were a trip to a resort in Cabo San Lucas.

Well, that Cabo vacation/root canal high came to an abrupt halt as soon as I arrived home, greeted by a child's most annoying question: "Can I play on your phone?"

I'd been away for hours, and when I stepped through the door, I didn't hear "Hi, Mommy!" or "I missed you!" Instead, it was straight-up, "Hey, gatekeeper of electronics? Gimme a fix."

My brain pulled a quote from *American Idol*'s Randy Jackson: "That's gonna be a no from me, dawg."

My husband and I had already noticed negative behaviors from the kids—extra sibling arguments, slowness to obey, difficulty concentrating, bursts of anger, general grumpiness. And heaven forbid when it was time to transition from a screen to not-a-screen . . . Yikes.

We would enforce consequences for these outbursts, but our kids' responses seemed almost primal. Something was changing internally. As if their little minds were shifting into fight-or-flight mode, completely different from their bright, spunky selves. The behaviors would come and go intermittently, so we wondered if it was an inevitable part of this wild ride we call parenthood.

We had no clue there was a deeper cause. We thought, *Hey, maybe acting like rivaling WWE wrestlers is normal for their ages.* We wondered if we needed to cut sugar out of their diets. Did they need more sleep? Less gluten? Boarding school? Holy water? We couldn't be sure.

We just knew that we didn't like it, and something had to change.

When my baby greeted me as if I was an electronics vending machine, that was the last straw. I called my husband at work.

"Babe. We need to pull the plug. The kids need a screen break."

"Awesome," he said. "Let's do it."

We broke the news to the kids that night at dinner. My husband made the announcement.

"Okay, kids. Until further notice, we are turning off all screens. There will be no Netflix, YouTube, Nintendo Switch, iPad, computer, Minecraft, Xbox. None. This is not negotiable. Do not bother asking us to play or watch anything screen related. We love you, and this is a change we are going to try out together. We need to unplug and reevaluate. We'll keep you posted."

Then we all hugged and celebrated a new beginning. Together, we made vision boards that forecasted a simpler time of family cultural enrichment, spending lazy days on the lawn, honing our basket-weaving skills.

Just kidding.

The kids immediately went into a state of mourning. You would have thought we told them our dog died. Tears abounded. For five minutes. Then we all moved on to the next topic.

But internally, I still feared what the next day would bring. I prepared for the worst—the children dressed in head-to-toe black, singing longingly, "Nobody knooooows the trouble I've seen. . . ."

What actually happened blew me away. The kids did not ask for one screen that day. They knew the topic would be a nonstarter. So instead, they played with the toys on their shelves. They played with each other. Lo and behold, they were already starting to act happier, more obedient, kinder, and overall, less addict-like. It was as if we had flipped an actual switch. As if we'd discovered some kind of miraculous parenting hack. I got my kids back. For us, it was that simple.

I hope that your detox is as simple as ours was. But be encouraged to know that if it isn't, you're not alone. I've helped coach many families through their own detoxes. Dual-working households. Homeschooling families. Foster families. Stay-at-home parents. Work-from-home parents. Big families. Small families. Of course, every family encountered unique levels of stress, complaining, and difficulty. In later chapters, you will hear many of their stories, trials, and triumphs. One family's first detox attempt failed a few hours in. But with some coaching and a new plan, they committed to a second try. And guess what? They were thrilled with their results. More on them in chapter 11. Of the families who used my plan and reported their results back to me, *100 percent experienced a dramatic and positive change by the end of two weeks.*

Am I guaranteeing that your journey will be easy? Not necessarily. But with some setup on the front end, it can be simple. And the obstacles you might encounter will be worth the momentary struggle. Guiding your kids through a digital detox is simple. And while it might not be easy, it will absolutely be worth it.

This decision will transform the culture of your home. You will be shocked that something so simple could change your family so profoundly.

At this point you might be wondering, how is it possible that digital entertainment is having such an enormous impact on our kids? How is this happening to amazing kids with great parents— especially if you are only allowing an hour or two of TV, tablets, and video games per day?

A totally different childhood

Today's parents feel the weight of an unprecedented amount of technology in the home, and the change has been gradual. It's not like a dam burst; it's more like our boats have been slowly taking on water. Another holiday brings a new console, a new iPhone, more video games. Another friend's parents allow a new app, and we feel the pressure to follow suit. These well-intentioned "gifts" are burying our kids in entertainment. We look around and see that everyone else seems to be parenting the same way. *Everyone can't be getting this wrong. If all kids are playing the games, if they're all on social media, then the status quo must be fine, right?* we wonder, as our boats continue to take on more water. Our kids are disengaged and ornery. Parents are frustrated. Our boats are sinking.

Seventy-eight percent of parents say that raising kids today is more complicated than when they grew up.[1] Eighty-five percent of parents are worried about the amount of time their kids are spending in front of a screen.[2] If technology is supposed to be so helpful, why is it stressing out parents and bringing out the worst in our kids?

From waking to bedtime, there's an app or a screen to fill the silences, the lulls, the boredom. And from a parent's perspective, it seems kind of great. Need to take a call? Hand over the iPad. Need a few minutes of peace and quiet on the long drive? Flip on a movie and hand the headphones to the back seat. But if you've been at this parenting gig for a few years and have taken advantage of these new options for kid entertainment, it doesn't take long to see the emotional and behavioral problems. Parents wonder, *Why does my child seamlessly transition from LEGO to puzzles, but the end of screen time turns her into a cave troll?* What is the cost of all this cheap and convenient entertainment?

We can't look to grandparents and great-grandparents for answers on this one. It's a massive, brand-new social experiment, and our kids are the guinea pigs.

Everything has changed

Yes, we all use technology daily for both productivity and diversion. But if you're reading this book, you probably spent the first decade plus of life learning how to be a human without screens (except television and movies), to be bored and troubleshoot and knock on the neighbor's door to find a friend. You had your feelings hurt and hurt someone else's. You learned how to make it right by apologizing, hugging it out, and moving on. You spent years honing the foundations of being in relationship with other people. With the extent technology is available to kids in our homes today, there's a diminished incentive for them to interact in real relationships.

There's no opportunity for the benefits of boredom. Easy entertainment is available to children in shiny rectangular boxes throughout the house. Why go outside? Why risk rejection by knocking on the neighbor's door? Why troubleshoot the uneven couch fort support mechanism? Why build anything? Why hone any skill? That would involve effort and setbacks. Why attempt any of the character-building, mind-forming activities that their parents' and grandparents' childhoods were built on?

So the kids don't. Not to the extent their brilliant little minds need. How can we blame them? If we grew up with the same diversions, we'd be doing the same thing. Some days we are. Parents get sucked into the entertainment vortex too.

The problem, it turns out, is that kids (and adults) are using screens as substitutes for face-to-face conversations. If you grew up in the 1980s and '90s like I did, then you remember. We built our middle school friendships over drippy Otter Pops and daisy chain necklaces. We endured conversational lulls required in any friendship worth building. We didn't have another option. And we reaped the relational fruit by investing time in the kids around us. We listened to friends confide about their parents' rocky marriages or their silly pets. We postulated how the world works from our weird ten-year-old brains. How will I escape when I inevitably fall into a pit of quicksand? (The greatest threat of childhood, according to third graders in the 1990s.) We strategized and wondered together, troubleshooting and laughing at inside jokes we created along the way. Our communication wasn't hindered by character limits. We had to interpret real body language and facial expressions, not ambiguous one-dimensional emojis.

We subconsciously understood that thousands of micro-interactions were the building blocks of budding relationships.

But now? Kids stare at screens. And the effects are starting to show in dramatic ways in the classroom, at the dinner table, at bedtime. Kids aren't developing the way they have for thousands of years.

How are screens putting my kids in a bad mood?

Ellie is fourteen. She had always been bright, fun, and friendly. But now she is exhausted all the time. She's often moody and lonely. When sad or bored, she picks up her phone and scrolls social media. "It helps me connect with my friends!" she tells her parents. They assume she is right, that this is how modern friendships work. They know that social connection is critical for teenagers, but Ellie still seems sad. In her social media world, Ellie scrolls through endless photos of flawless filtered teenagers. Why can't she look like them? Her "friends" tease her on group text about her crush. Someone screenshots their conversation and sends it to the target of her secret affection. Ellie is mortified.

In years past, she went to the kitchen and talked with Mom. Now she puts on her headphones and numbs out on TikTok. Two hours later, it's time for dinner and she hasn't started her homework. She comes to the dinner table feeling dejected and ugly, but Mom and Dad see it as "typical teenage attitude." They haven't seen Ellie all day and want to hear how she's doing, but she's moody and snaps at them when they try. Ellie heads back to her room to scroll social media in front of the blank Word document that is supposed to be her history paper. It's ten p.m. Mom checks on Ellie to see her headphones on and history book open, and concludes that kids are under way too much pressure at school these days.

Data shows that teens are more anxious, depressed, and suicidal than ever before. As one high school teacher told me, "Parents assume that if a child is quiet and in their room, that must mean they're okay. . . . But they're not okay."

What about younger kids?

Ever turn off the tablet or video game only to watch your precious angel morph into a deranged lunatic? There's more going on than a simple tantrum.

Video games, smartphone games, tablet games, social media platforms—they are all deliberately designed to trigger the release of dopamine, a chemical in our brains that makes us feel good.

"When dopamine rises and falls suddenly . . . the child can become weepy, impulsive, or angry. It's as though the sudden fall in dopamine causes the brain to short circuit; every little demand on the child becomes stressful. Since dopamine is needed to execute tasks, when it's suddenly low, every task becomes overwhelming, setting the stage for a meltdown,"[3] explains child psychiatrist Dr. Victoria Dunckley. Aha! Your child isn't *trying* to impersonate Linda Blair in *The Exorcist* when the iPad timer dings. Science shows us that electronic devices are chemically priming our kids' brains to respond with the rage and furor of a scorned Real Housewife.

Is sleep actually affected by screen usage? Even if it is, does that really matter?

Cynthia noticed that her three young kids were moody and irritable—almost daily. She wondered if this was normal for their ages—three, five, and seven. She was a conscientious mother who limited her children to two hours of video-game play per day. Cynthia had no idea that her kids' game play was interfering with their sleep quality. As soon as she digitally detoxed her children, their moodiness problems nearly vanished.

Toddlers, kids, and teens who use tablets, video games, and social media during the day take longer to fall asleep and have more disruptive nighttime sleep.[4] Poor sleep quality then creates a terrible cycle: tired kids are moody kids. They can't focus, they are more stressed, and in turn, they can't sleep. And then they crave even more stimulation. Studies have also shown that teens who use their phones after lights-out have significantly increased risks for mental health problems, suicidal feelings, and self-injury.[5]

One psychotherapist says that 80 percent of his patients' issues are a result of excessive screen use. Dr. George Lynn describes this as "a personality syndrome that comes from basically unbridled, uncontrolled recreational use of screen media during the day and at night. . . . Most doctors, family doctors, even psychiatric practitioners are not hip to the obvious fact that a kid might be only getting two to three hours of sleep at night if that. . . . And that causes personality problems."[6]

How much time are kids actually spending on screens?

Almost half of two- to four-year-old children and more than two-thirds of five- to eight-year-olds have their own tablet or smartphone.[7] Five- to eight-year-olds are using screen-based entertainment more than three hours per day.[8] Eight- to twelve-year-old kids are using six hours of media entertainment per day. Recreational screen time for twelve- and thirteen-year-olds doubled over the course of the COVID-19 pandemic, from nearly four hours per day to nearly eight. This, even after kids returned to in-person learning.[9] Thirteen- to eighteen-year-olds are spending *nine hours per day* consuming entertainment media.[10] This does not include screens used for schoolwork. *That is the majority of a child's waking life.*

My child seems extra focused when he uses his tablet. Doesn't that mean it's teaching him how to focus?

On the outside, it might appear that kids are laser focused while tapping away. "Look at my little Einstein!" Mom beams. The truth is that digital entertainment is eroding your child's ability to concentrate. Instead, it's overstimulating him with novel distractions. Shiny object! Bright colors! Loud sounds! Screen time often thrusts our youngest kids into a continuously hyperattentive state. Their brains are soaking in cortisol and adrenaline, the fight, flight, and stress hormones. This results in our kids "first passively receiving and then . . . actively requiring" excessive levels of stimulation.[11]

When your child appears quiet and calm in the glow of his device, his brain might be in fight-or-flight mode. No wonder he snaps when you tell him screen time is over.

What if my kids only spend an hour per day on screens? Is that okay?

Let's say you limit your child's screen use to one or two hours per day. Sounds reasonable. . . . But think of the proportion of free time that those two hours comprise. A ten-year-old wakes up at seven a.m., gets dressed, and goes to school until three p.m. From three to four he has baseball practice. From four to five he finishes his homework. He eats dinner with his family from five to six, helps with dishes until six-thirty, then plays Wack a Mole Simulator from six-thirty to eight-thirty. This typical child has two hours of free, unscheduled time during his weekdays before bedtime, and he is spending 100 percent of it playing a video game. Do we want our kids spending a majority of their free time consuming digital entertainment? That would leave exactly zero time for riding bikes with friends, building tree forts, reading for pleasure, watching planes fly overhead from the trampoline, interacting with the neighbor kid, shooting the breeze with Dad at the kitchen table. Even if our kids are spending an hour per day, there are substantial opportunity costs.

But we grew up watching TV and playing Nintendo in the '80s and '90s. Isn't today's digital entertainment the same thing, but for the next generation?

Not even close.

The kind of digital entertainment available to our kids is like nothing we've seen in generations past. Neurological experts have closely studied the way that the brain releases dopamine as a response to pleasurable experiences: a hug, smelling a flower, riding a bicycle. Tech engineers have used this research to bake dopamine release points into their apps, video games, and social media platforms. They have studied the frequency and type of rewards that hook people to their products. It's the same tactics casinos use. Experts are paid to keep kids scrolling and playing. And they're

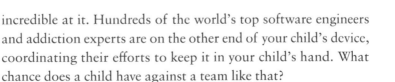

Studies continue to demonstrate that children are susceptible to health, behavioral, cognitive, and developmental problems related to certain types of digital media use. Those risks include

delayed language development
difficulty processing emotional signals
internet/gaming addiction
reduced memory capacity
depression
anxiety
sleep disorders
reduced level of text comprehension
ADHD diagnoses
lower empathy
lower literacy abilities
lower executive function
hampered deep-reading abilities
aggressive behaviors
lowered levels of prosocial behavior
difficulty storing relevant facts
irritability
impulsivity
reduced social skills
difficulty with solitude
vision problems
underdeveloped emotional regulation skills
avoidance of social interaction

incredible at it. Hundreds of the world's top software engineers and addiction experts are on the other end of your child's device, coordinating their efforts to keep it in your child's hand. What chance does a child have against a team like that?

As if that weren't enough, the constant dopamine surges in kids' brains are so huge that dopamine receptors are numbing out.

Now these little ones need even more dopamine in order to feel the same amount of pleasure they previously enjoyed. Bearing this level of arousal in mind, we can understand why simply looking at how many hours your kids are on screens is not the whole story. Dopamine is flowing like Niagara Falls in those young minds. The combination of parental permission and tech availability is creating tech-hooked kids. The long-term effects of excessive screen use include increased risk of depression, anxiety, negative thinking, coping difficulties, lack of resilience, and even heart disease.[12]

This is not 1980s Pac-Man games and *Little House on the Prairie*. This is new technology, brilliantly engineered to suck your kids in. One hour of today's screens is not the same as one hour of Saturday morning cartoons when you were a kid.

New health problems

So what does this have to do with your first grader's tantrums? Occupational therapists are observing more children who exhibit autism-like behaviors but are not, in fact, autistic. They are calling this "virtual autism," because it is caused by too much screen use and not enough sensory play.[13] Increased screen time in young kids impairs language development and mood, and induces autistic-like behavior, including hyperactivity, short attention span, and irritability.[14] Does this sound familiar?

ADHD diagnoses are on the rise. What are symptoms of ADHD, according to Mayo Clinic? Hyperactivity, impulsivity, short attention span, avoiding tasks that require effort, appearing not to listen, becoming easily distracted, fidgeting. Parents, does this sound eerily similar to a seven-year-old coming off a two-hour Fortnite bender?

Child psychiatrist Dr. Dunckley believes that a common environmental stressor is to blame for this explosion of so-called diagnoses. In fact, she has named a new disorder as the culprit: Electronic Screen Syndrome (ESS). It makes kids unable to control their moods, attention, or excitement in a socially appropriate way. ESS can create or worsen ADHD, depression, oppositional defiant disorder, and anxiety. Signs of ESS include irritable, depressed, or rapidly changing moods, excessive or age-inappropriate tantrums, low frustration tolerance, poor self-regulation, poor sportsmanship, poor eye contact, and learning difficulties.[15]

Educators on the front lines

George Petersen is an accomplished principal of a Blue Ribbon School and was recognized as one of the nation's top ten principals in 2019. I was interested to hear what he was seeing on the front lines at his local school.

What he shared with me was fascinating and alarming.

"More students are struggling with normal social situations. In the classroom, students appear to be less resilient with academic rigor and more frustrated with collaborative learning. They are more easily distracted and less likely to take risks," he said.

What's to blame for this noticeable decline? Socioeconomic status? Nope. The problem educators are seeing "cuts across demographics," according to Mr. Petersen.

So what's the problem?

"As my staff and I intervene with students who struggle, we are finding a common theme: 'I play on my tablet four hours a day,' 'My parents allow me to be on YouTube when they're not home,' 'After school, I play video games all afternoon.' Earning points by blowing up a building on a computer screen will produce a greater dopamine release than solving a math problem. When children live in isolation, self-absorbed in the world of technology, they do not practice how to socially, emotionally, and verbally interact with one another in a healthy manner. Taking turns with play equipment and listening respectfully to a partner in a group have become extremely difficult tasks for many students. Students fall further behind when their home lives are absorbed by a screen."[16]

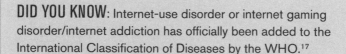

DID YOU KNOW: Internet-use disorder or internet gaming disorder/internet addiction has officially been added to the International Classification of Diseases by the WHO.[17]

I'd been reading about these situations and had already noticed worrisome behaviors from my kids at home. But now one of the country's top principals confirmed it—ours was not an isolated incident. It's happening everywhere.

Screens are impacting all of our kids in the worst ways. Mr. Petersen wasn't only talking about "difficult" children or uninvolved parents. He was talking about all kids. Kids from strong families. Great kids with great parents, navigating the world where digital entertainment is everywhere. We are all trying to parent through difficult behaviors, without realizing that an external component has a hold on our kids. We can't compete with the way screens are affecting their brains. This isn't the kids' fault. They are simply human beings responding to stimuli that were designed to keep them playing, watching, using.

The impact of their screen time is going far beyond screen time. It's changing the way kids think, interact with peers, respond to teachers. It's changing their ability to connect with other humans.

What does the future look like for kids raised on excessive digital entertainment?

What happens when kids replace face-to-face, human-to-human connection with screens? Parents today have a unique vantage point. The first generation of kids who grew up with a smartphone in hand has graduated college and begun their work in the real world. Employers report that this generation is coming to work with new phobias and anxieties. "They don't know how to begin and end conversations. They have a hard time with eye contact.

They say that talking on the telephone makes them anxious," according to MIT professor and psychologist Sherry Turkle. "It is worth asking a hard question: Are we unintentionally depriving our children of tools they need at the very moment they need them? Are we depriving them of skills that are crucial to friendship, creativity, love, and work?"[18]

So what should we do?

That's it. We're becoming Amish. (Can you still color your hair and use a curling iron if you're Amish? No? Okay, scratch the Amish thing.)

We see what screen time is doing to the kids. But do we need to summarily dump every form of technology because some of it is harmful? Is there any way to harness the best parts of screens and tech without the kids morphing into *The Walking Dead: Kindergarten Edition*?

The answer is absolutely yes. There is a way. And it looks different in each household. The good news is that you're the parent, you know your children best, and you get to decide what your family's relationship with screens is going to look like in your own home.

We don't have to move off the grid and grow all of our own food and throw out our curling irons. (The horror!) Used rightly, technology can serve us as a helpful sidekick on this wild and crazy life. Rather than banning all of it forever, we want our relationship with tech to be like maintaining a healthy diet.

A lifetime of twice-a-day Twinkies and Dr. Pepper will nearly ensure chronic health problems. Similarly, decades of tech for entertainment will stunt our kids' emotional, intellectual, and social development. Just because the grocery stores are filled with processed foods and sugar doesn't mean we should buy it. And just because our kids have access to endless screens for entertainment doesn't mean they should use them.

Cheap tech for entertainment has flooded into our homes so quickly over the last decade, we haven't had a chance to catch our breath. We haven't stopped for a moment to say, "Is this best? Does this further our family's purpose? Do all these toys further our vision for our long-term parenting plan? Do we even have a long-term parenting plan?"

How does tech fit with your family's purpose?

On a bad day, in the midst of tantrums and carpool, it can feel like we're mustering every ounce of effort to survive until bedtime. On those days, we view screens as a momentary respite for Mom or Dad, despite knowing the long-term effects on our kids' behavior. But I don't want to "survive" until the kids move out. What a waste of years with our beloved children. What is our destination? Let's clarify that, and then decide how technology fits into our household from that thirty-thousand-foot view of parenthood.

What do you want to accomplish with your kids during these short years? Step back and decide. These will be your family's guiding principles.

For example, here are our family's guiding principles:

- We teach our kids that our first priorities as a family are to love God and love people.
- In a world prioritizing individual comfort and ease, you will have to reject both—often—in order to love God and love people.
- If we want our kids to believe this is true and worthwhile, we need to model this as parents every day. Some days we fall woefully short, and that leads us to the next point. . . .
- When we mess up, we own it.
- Each person is wired a little differently with gifts and quirks. How can we discover our kids' gifts and help share those with others?

- Over the lifetime of your relationship with your children, you will both be adults for the majority of those years. You'll share an adult-to-adult relationship from your kids' early twenties on. There is plenty of time for that kind of mutual relationship. But for now, for these few years, our job is to discipline and train up kids, creating loving and firm parameters. We are seeing the fruit of this with our older kids, watching our roles transition from authority to coach. But in order to best love our kids as they grow, we are not their BFFs. We are their parents.

How would you answer your big-picture goals for your family? What are your guiding principles?

They don't need to be fancy. Picture having lunch with your future eighteen-year-old child, the day you are moving him into his dorm room, sending him out into the world to make his own choices. You ask him, "Looking back, what principles guided our home? Based on how our home operated, both what we taught you and how we lived?" In your detox journal, write what you hope he would say. This is an important first step that sets the foundation for the digital detox, which I will guide you through on the pages ahead.

We have our guiding principles. Now what?

When you come out on the other side of this thing, you will have a clearer understanding of how to partner with technology so that it is a household tool. We are no longer okay with feeling like our kids are enslaved to tech. With your family's purpose and goals in mind, let's wade through the deluge of technology for kids. How should we proceed on a daily basis?

Now it is time to step back. For two weeks, in a digital detox. An elimination diet. A reset button. This is easier than you imagine and will yield better results than you could hope.

You might be thinking, *Wait a minute, I thought you said that some screens were okay.* Yes! After the detox, you will make a long-term plan for your kids and your home, and I would guess that plan will include family movie nights and more. But right now, your kids need some space from screens to rekindle nonscreen interests and redevelop their boredom-negotiation skills.

As you follow the four simple steps to a successful digital detox, you'll read about fellow parents' successes, hurdles, and tips along the way. I'll share our family's long-term technology plan and the long-term plans of several other families, and help you create your own, specifically tailored for your unique family.

You are not in this alone, and the path forward is surprisingly simple. It all starts with two weeks, and four simple steps:

UNDO THE TECH TRANCE

Unplug cold turkey.
Notice your kids' interests, talents, opportunities for growth.
Develop a list of screen-free fun together.
Open the books!

PART ONE

UNDO
THE
TECH TRANCE

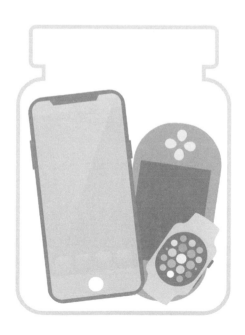

2

Unplug Cold Turkey

By the age of seven years, a child born today will have spent one full year of 24 [hour] days watching screen media.

DR. ARIC SIGMAN

MADISON WAS FIFTEEN. She was in foster care and needed a home. Foster parents Julie and John said yes to the placement, and were so glad they did. "Madison was friendly, kind to our kids, and openly shared her thoughts and questions about life," Julie told me with a smile. "We'd find her drawing at our kitchen table, playing games on the trampoline with our younger kids, or creating dance routines with them."

Julie and John grew close with Madison very quickly. "She opened up to us about her life and fears, favorite hobbies, funny stories," John recounted. One day, Madison's social worker moved her to a different home, which happens in foster care for a variety of reasons. When Madison returned to their home a few months later, she brought a laptop and smartphone with her.

"She was the same child, of course—fun, interesting, kind. But she didn't leave her room much. I never found her at the kitchen table. She would leave our family movie to sit in her room on her own computer. Instead of conversation happening naturally, I'd have to go into her room to hang out, but I was competing with the draw of her glowing screen. We didn't enjoy half of the relational connection we had during her first stay with us," Julie told me.

The differences in these two separate stays were stark. Madison's first stay allowed for deep connection, the second did not. The only difference? The availability of screen entertainment.

I was already a true believer in the power of unplugging our kids from devices because I'd seen the positive transformation in my own five children. But Julie and John's story of Madison's juxtaposing stays is a powerful reminder that screens can suffocate connection.

Your digital detox will be like a relational defibrillator, reawakening connection with your kids.

Do we really need to remove ALL screens?

In short, yes.

I know your stress, because I felt it too. Before we started, I assumed the process was going to suck the life out of me. I imagined that I'd become a triage nurse, overseeing a house of screen addicts going through withdrawal. I envisioned a bleak scene: weeping and wailing kids, unable to think of an independent play activity. I imagined every mom task would be met with five sets of eyes gawking at me, like those creepy little girls from *The Shining*, waiting for instructions. Asking for another snack.

Does the idea of banning all screens cold turkey create a similar scene in your brain? Maybe warning signs have been popping up for some time, continually hinting that it's time for a break. Perhaps the bleak visions of bored and whiny children prevent you from pulling the trigger on your actual digital detox.

It took me months to finally commit to such a radical change, because I know what all modern parents know: Screens are a magic weapon for Mom and Dad. If the kids can't seem to hush for that important phone call, turn on the Xbox, and voilà! An instant electronic babysitter.

Banishing the "babysitter" might sound more like punishing Mom than helping the kids. But it won't take long to realize that your fears of a total boredom wasteland were a figment of your imagination. In fact, reality may prove the opposite.

Truth be told, many kids *enjoy* the screenless time. I've helped a lot of families detox their kids. Most parents report that their kids shift into a kinder, gentler, and more cooperative attitude, almost immediately. You will not have the kind of life-changing results you are looking for if you simply cut the screen time short, instead of taking away all of it. Total removal is a critical part of the detox, the bedrock on which your results rest. Here's why:

- If kids know that a video game or tablet time awaits them, they will not be as focused on other activities, connections, or creating. They will simply be passing time until their window of screen usage pops up. This is because everyday activities cannot compete with the level of dopamine (the chemical surge of good feelings) released by tech entertainment.

- You are creating a two-week observation zone to watch your kids without any technology at all. You're going to become a student of your kids, carefully noticing the talents and skills that draw them in during lulls. To observe your kids most clearly, you need to remove all of the screens.

- A cold-turkey removal of screens will best equip you at the end of the detox, when you are creating your family's new, long-term plan. You can't really assess which types of technology are indispensable until you have removed them all.

- You've observed external behaviors in your kids that you don't like: grumpiness, angry outbursts when screen time

41

ends. But the impact of screens is not only external. Brain MRI scans have revealed physical changes when kids are using screens. When you remove all screens for entertainment, you are giving your kids and their brains a fresh start.

When your computer is glitching, the first suggested fix is always to restart it. Any IT guy at any help desk will advise you exactly the same way: Press that reset button. Well, these two weeks are a way for you to press the technology reset button for your family. There are some household "glitches" that warrant a reboot. In the long run, two weeks is a miniscule amount of time to turn off the screens. But it is just enough to clean the slate and start fresh. An opportunity for you and your spouse to huddle, observe, and implement best practices for your current parenting season, tailored for each individual child. It will be a tech reset that your kids will learn to love.

Life-giving benefits of a screens break: opportunities to connect

When you visit a friend, you exchange pleasantries, put down your bag, take off your shoes, grab a muffin, and talk about the air quality. It's a full fifteen minutes before you're covering the nitty-gritty: your dad's cancer diagnosis, your son's student council victory, your terrible calendar-keeping skills and the resulting encounter with your child's therapist at your front door while in your bathrobe.

It's been suggested that it takes seven minutes to see how a conversation will unfold.[1] Seven minutes of chitchat about the weather before people pivot to heart-level discussion—the real stuff. The doubts and affections scampering about your brain, they don't spill out right away. The good stuff takes a little coercing, a little massaging.

We all have a billion complex thoughts and emotions running around inside our heads. They need an opportunity to come out so we can process with a loved one. We need to share our burdens, because we need help carrying them. When we share victories, the celebrations are amplified. And don't you love sharing those mom-fail moments? Somehow verbalizing them to a friend switches the entire experience from mortifying to hilarious. This gold only happens when we are connecting with people. It's how human beings are wired: We need connection in order to thrive. Our kids are the same.

When your tiny people hop off the school bus, sweaty and hungry, scarf a snack, and then flip on Netflix, they miss opportunities for longer conversations with Mom or Dad, the kind that open a door to how school *really* was.

The cafeteria served a chicken patty in the shape of California, a nervous child visited the nurse for a strange red mark (turned out to be Crayola), and the crush asked to borrow a pencil! These gems never come pouring out right when they get home from school. Our kids need to take off their shoes, put down their bag, grab a snack, and exhale. Not to be interviewed, but to be parented.

We're their safe space. Our kitchen tables are havens for connection. But when easy entertainment beckons them from the tablet or the game console, you'd better believe they'll go running there first. We all do. It's no one's fault, but it is a newish facet of modern parenting. If we aren't careful, we can miss out on something fundamental and sacred: slow conversations, shooting the breeze, and listening to what comes out of our kids' hearts. Their profound concern for animals or foster kids or space exploration.

How often do you and your kids sit and talk with each other in chunks of time longer than seven minutes, without anyone checking a phone or email or glancing at the TV?

The total removal of all screens for entertainment will provide new opportunities for connecting with your favorite people on earth. My kitchen went from empty during meal prep (thanks to their daily hour of screen time) to bustling (thanks to our detox). When screens were simply not an option, all of my kids began to spend this hour in the heart of the home.

COACHING TIP: Recruit a buddy! Talk to a friend or neighbor about detoxing your kids simultaneously. The benefits of the buddy system include

- mutual encouragement
- accountability
- playdate buddies
- commiseration partner
- troubleshooting common problems together
- reminding each other that the sacrifice is worth it!

They drew pictures and listened to stories. They retold jokes heard at school. They asked about cooking techniques. And during silent lulls, one wondered aloud about how to help the sad kid at school, another shared their own trouble with friends. These glimpses into their vulnerable hearts are priceless, and they will be plentiful during your digital detox.

My guess is that you already are a conscientious parent. (After all, you did buy this book!) But even if you are only allowing for an hour of screens per day, like we were before our detox, you will be blown away when you see how a total removal of technology for entertainment increases opportunities for connecting with your kids.

Distracted connecting: the myth of multitasking

One Sunday afternoon I was playing a board game with our four-year-old foster daughter at a friend's house. She'd lived with us for two years and had grown by leaps and bounds. She was naturally very intelligent, but sitting still and focusing on one activity were difficult. About a year after our detox, when screen entertainment was no longer part of their daily lives, we lay on the carpet, taking turns with the board game Trouble. We each rolled the dice, and then counted how many spaces to move. We enjoyed eye contact, smiles, and even some giggles.

I remember treasuring up the minutes with her, because it was such intensive opportunity for connection. I marveled at her growth. The little girl who previously couldn't focus was now playing a game that was made for kids older than she was. This was a massive victory.

After about ten minutes of play, someone walked in from another room and flipped on the TV. Her eyes shot up at the screen, sucked in. In an instant I lost her. We still tried to take turns, but I now had to inform her every time she needed to roll. I went from having 100 percent of her attention—which opened the door to heart connection—to having maybe 15 percent of her attention. She was getting bored of the game, and I was frustrated. It took me a minute to realize how quickly the setup had shifted, and how all of that was within my control as the parent. I turned off the TV, and we resumed our board game with the focus and connection we'd had before.

The juxtaposition between my daughter's available attention with a TV on in the background and without was alarming. Research has shown this to be true across the board—background television reduces the length of time a child plays and a child's focused attention during play.[2] We have all become so accustomed to our kids' splintered attention. Until our detox, I didn't even notice how profound the comparison was. I didn't fully grasp how strong a hold screens had on my kids. Not until we removed them all.

After enjoying the tremendous results of our digital detox, I had a million questions. Could happier, easier parenting be as simple as turning off the screens? Why is something as pervasive as screen technology having this negative impact on our day-to-day lives? Certainly, technology can be useful and even helpful in connecting with people we love most. But so often it gets in the way. How do we figure out best practices so that its role is more helpful than harmful?

My kids' detox challenged my beliefs about the benefits of multitasking. I have come to believe that multitasking is not as productive or beneficial as unitasking. (Which is apparently so uncommon that my spell check refuses to accept it as an actual word.)

As a mother of many, multitasking has always been my jam. I bet you can relate. Nursing a baby while sautéing dinner *and* quizzing a child on spelling words *and* moderating a LEGO property dispute *and* listening to a podcast. Multitasking is my life.

I assumed my kids would follow in the footsteps of their mother, and all for the sake of productivity. Right? Wrong. Apparently, multitasking is actually just our brains bouncing quickly from thing to thing, like clicking through several internet browser tabs. Our performance degrades with each new task added. But why does multitasking feel productive? Because it gives us a neuro-chemical high—so we think we're doing better, but in reality, we are doing worse. Multitasking also hinders our ability to read human emotions.[3]

As modern parents, we have all seen the distracted look in our kids' eyes when they are attempting any task or conversation while simultaneously engaged in tech entertainment. This is not unique to our children. And it doesn't necessarily mean they are addicted. It simply means we need to be aware enough to respect the power of screens.

One psychologist notes that the path forward is to learn more about our vulnerabilities regarding technology, and then use that information to design the most helpful environments. For our family, we want the technology working for us, rather than us being enslaved to it. This is what the digital detox will help you do: observe and determine how and in which contexts you will allow technology in your own home.

You might find that the hour per day of screen time after school is not as necessary for your sanity as you'd assumed. Your kids may even say that they enjoy the reprieve from being forced to respond to thousands of text messages from their friends, like one fourteen-year-old did after her own detox.

When she turned on her phone after a two-week break, fourteen-year-old Ava discovered *four thousand* text messages from her friends. After reading through them, she said she didn't miss anything of consequence. Initially hesitant about the detox, Ava shared she was ultimately grateful for the break.

An opportunity to negotiate boredom

Another invaluable aspect of the total-tech ban: opportunities for kids to experience boredom. Many parents view boredom as a problem to be solved. But teachers and psychologists explain that boredom is not a problem, it's an opportunity. Boredom is your imagination beckoning you to create, to invent. This is an important skill for our kids to learn early.

When I was in high school, my group of friends could have fun anytime, anywhere—without any illegal substances. Give us a trash can lid and a hill, and we would laugh for hours. With a pad of paper and a jar, we would play charades into the wee hours of the morning. These were kids who grew up in the 1980s and '90s. They encountered boredom head-on, wondered how to make do with their surroundings, and whipped up some fun. They caught lizards and knocked on the neighbor's door to play. They invented clubs and dug holes to China. While spending time with these friends, never was the word *bored* uttered. These teens had spent their early years negotiating their own boredom. I'm still friends with these wonderful people, and they are interesting, thoughtful adults.

When you remove the crutch of passive entertainment from your kids, you give them the opportunity to be alone with their creativity. Their imaginations and hidden talents are inside, ready to burst. Too often, their creativity lies dormant, numbed out on a glowing screen. But not during your digital detox. For these two weeks, you're removing the filter, creating a space for the back-and-forth of their imagination to ruminate, to ponder the flowers and clouds. They will mull on their interests and curiosities, troubleshooting and problem-solving. This skill is foundational to becoming successful, relational adults.

One morning during our detox, my five kids made a couch fort city in the living room. I overheard them establishing their own form of local government, a library, and even a city-wide mayoral election. After distributing paper ballots, the kids all wrote the name of the sibling they wished to elect. (Except my four-year-old daughter, who requested that I write the name Alexa on her ballot. She was casting her vote for our home's electronic assistant. After the kids cleared up that all candidates must be humans, the election reconvened.)

The mayor-elect announced that the town would host happy hour. All five kids cheered, while I nervously wondered why my kids were rejoicing at the term . . . until the mayor clarified: "Happy hour means that the library is open for an additional hour today!" The room erupted in applause.

Five kids, ages four to ten, played cooperatively like this—for three hours. This would not have happened with a mere reduction of screen time. One or more of the kids would have lost interest, asking to play a game or watch a show. Instead, with screens out of the picture, the kids hit a boredom wall and then troubleshot ways to solve it: an election, happy hour, a new fort feature.

Like every loving parent, I always knew my kids were wonderful. But I didn't fully appreciate the extent of their creativity—until they were forced to use it. The kids created an entire system of currency out of different types of rocks they found in the yard. My seven-year-old launched a comic book club, where he teaches his siblings how to create their own comic books.

One day, my four-year-old desperately wanted somebody to paint her nails. I was busy cooking dinner. My son walked in, saw the need, and happily volunteered to do the manicure himself.

If he'd had the option of playing his favorite video game at that moment, there is no way he would have painted his sister's nails instead. The two of them bonded over which colors and how many coats. He felt valued and helpful, and little sister was beaming.

I've treasured these scenes in my heart, but they are far from remarkable. They are simply **what any and all kids will do if they don't have the option to be sucked into easy, mindless entertainment.** Watch how much more clearly you begin to see your kids' natural giftings and interests when they aren't numbing out on a device. Unplugging cold turkey, even for only two weeks, will force your kids to reach into those creative places to invent and imagine.

New opportunities for honing interests and sibling bonding

Two weeks into screen detox mode, sisters Brielle and Halle, ages four and eight, were playing cooperatively like never before. Their mom, Marissa, reported that the two girls had spent an entire three-day weekend playing with Barbies, board games, card games, backyard swings, and more. Brielle didn't often initiate play before their digital detox, but now she was asking Halle to play and taking the time to teach her new games.

Mom Sharon reported that one day in the middle of their family's digital detox, she was so tired she considered turning on some old movies for her three kids. When she went to check on them, she found them reading books to each other and then making a bunk bed fort. Sharon felt reenergized because her kids took the initiative to create a worthwhile activity on their own.

For years, our nine-year-old son had expressed interest in cooking. But it wasn't until our full-fledged screen removal that he chose to sit in the kitchen for extended periods of time, asking for more and more responsibility. After lots of practice, he now occasionally asks to make lunch for all of his siblings. During busy days, I even assign him this job as a way to serve the family. Quesadillas are his specialty, and you should see his face light up when the tableful of family tastes and unanimously approves.

Any of these activities and skills are available to our kids when screens are an option. But the magnetic pull of electronic entertainment is simply too strong. If parents aren't intentional in their approach to technology in the home, screen entertainment will replace priceless hours of childhood when kids need to imagine, create, and connect.

No doubt after your detox, you will allow a specified amount of electronic devices into your home. But at that point, you'll have a clearer understanding of how your kids are wired, plus the types and extent of screen time that is beneficial versus harmful to them. You are only able to observe this once you remove all electronic entertainment for your kids. I know it sounds hard, but you can do this!

Exceptions to screen detox rules

Remember the movie *Bird Box*? It is a sci-fi thriller in which Sandra Bullock tries to protect herself and two children from horrible creatures that live outside. Anyone who lays eyes on the creatures is immediately doomed. For this reason, Sandra, her kids, and all other humans wear blindfolds whenever they go outside. To be without a blindfold is to die.

Your digital detox is not *Bird Box*. If you are eating at a restaurant with your kids and there's a baseball game on the TV, if cartoons are playing in the pediatrician's waiting room, if your kids are headed to a friend's house for a playdate and the mom who's hosting has planned an outdoor movie—no big deal. A one-off outside of your home will not derail your technology reset. Don't stress about random exceptions that are outside of your control.

The detox is set up to work *for* you, to give you clarity and find your purpose for technology in your home. Don't let it stress you out. Done right, it will be life-giving and informative. Here are other reasonable exceptions we made during our detox, and exceptions friends had to make that did not impact their results at all:

- One of our kids had an appointment with a speech therapist through a virtual meeting. We did not cancel his appointment to avoid using electronics.
- Another child was homeschooled, and his math curriculum was through an online textbook. We still allowed our son to do his math schoolwork even though it was through an electronic device.
- We allowed any teacher-led classroom activity that relied on electronics. We did not march into the school and request a special exemption for our child because of a new detox we were trying out at home. (If you think your school is relying too heavily on screen time, it is absolutely worth a conversation with your child's teacher and possibly principal. But I suggest waiting until after your detox is complete.)

But remember, you are doing your best to create a tech-detoxing space for two full weeks. So don't allow "screens required for school" to include the use of any educational app at home. (Admittedly, living in an increasingly digital world can blur lines around where education stops and entertainment begins. More help on this in chapter 10, "Tech and Learning.") While you are at home, it should be simple to monitor this. And you should feel comfortable telling your paid babysitters that movies, TV shows, and video games are not allowed. These nannies and babysitters are a valuable and integral part of your family. They should be able to accommodate your requests. Day care might be a different story, but talk to your day-care provider and ask if they have any thoughts or ideas. You are all on the same team, working to help your kids grow and learn.

YOU CAN'T KNOW the extent that screen time is impacting your kids until you observe their baseline, with zero screen entertainment. Going cold turkey allows you to see this baseline.

Parents Jarod and Marissa implemented a digital detox for their four kids, ages four to thirteen. One night, Grandma and Grandpa watched the kids while Mom and Dad enjoyed a date night. The kids loved to spend the night at Grandma and Grandpa's house, which usually included TV time. But Marissa told her parents about their detox and asked if they would be willing to oversee a different activity. Her parents were on board. Instead of mindlessly watching a movie, which would soon be forgotten, the four kids worked together with their grandparents on a project: cleaning out the attic. Not surprisingly, the kids were bummed at the prospect. But by the time they were finished, the kids and grandparents had made lasting memories and were grateful for the time well spent.

Breaking the news to the kids

Your attitude and posture in this conversation are everything. So before you break the news to the kids, make sure you and your spouse are on the same page. If it takes time to talk out your plan, and *get* on the same page first, that's totally fine. You want to be a united front. Once you've arrived at your plan, *then* tell the kids. If they're going to attempt a coup, Mom and Dad need to be allied and ready.

There will be tears. Remember, you are doing this for their good. You love your kids and it's your job to raise them well, feeding their hearts, souls, and minds. You've clearly arrived at your decision out of deep affection for them. And while you are going to be empathetic to their momentary sadness, remember that they can't see the end results right now. They're looking at the short-term loss. You have the benefit of the long-term vision: future adults who are well-adjusted and kind, know how to be bored without collapsing in despair, and know how to connect with others. You are clearing the path for them. You are creating a space for clarity so you can help them navigate a new technological world. You are giving them a gift. Don't be deterred by their tears. Instead, remember that you can see more of the picture than they can.

Do not apologize for the detox. Present it as something new and worthwhile your family is going to try for a short time.

Here is one method you can use: Gather your people together over a meal or dessert and say, "Hey, we're going to try something new for a little while. We've read about the benefits of taking a technology break, and have read about other families who have tried it with great results. We want our family to enjoy time together without any screens. So we're going to take a screen break. It won't be forever, but for now, you guys will not be using any electronic devices. I know it can be hard to take a break from something you enjoy, but we believe this is going to be good for our family. We start tomorrow."

This is essentially what we told our kids. Their despair and sobbing only lasted for about five minutes. We listened empathetically to their objections and questions, but remained firm and loving in our decision. We didn't present it as a punishment for anything, but as an opportunity to try something new. After a few minutes, we all moved on to the next topic. By the time morning rolled around, they had already come to terms with the idea and, surprisingly, did not complain at all.

For our kids, this initial conversation was the hardest part of the detox. Once you get past this, you can do anything. But that's only going to be true if you stick to your decision. If you're wishy-washy or cave at the first sign of their disappointment, you'll only be making your life more difficult and rendering the detox ineffective. So make sure you are ready to jump in, and then go for it!

One note: I am asked all the time if my husband and I also detoxed from screens along with the kids. The answer is no, and for a few reasons.

First, when parents impose a rule on their kids, that doesn't mean the parents must follow the exact same rules. For example, if you enforce an eight p.m. bedtime for the kids, do you and your spouse feel obliged to do the same for yourselves? No, you are adults, and they are children. You choose your own bedtime.

Second, as parents, we are using our phones to take care of business: grocery shopping, banking, scheduling medical appointments. The hope is that, as adults, you understand how and when to limit your tech use, and you recognize what is helpful versus what is hindering your presence and productivity. (Although I did eventually detox myself. But more on this in chapter 12, "Tech for Mom and Dad.")

It is completely your decision whether you join your kids in their digital detox. But remember, the way we *model* appropriate tech use will teach our children more than what we *tell* them about how they should use it. Mom Marissa did a social media detox alongside her kids' tech detox as a gesture of solidarity. Gauge your kids' and your own tech usage, and make a decision that works best for your family.

Fourteen days is going to be easier than you'd think. You'll need this time to fully implement the rest of the plan. These two weeks have the potential to change your life.

BEFORE YOU BEGIN CHECKLIST

☐ Talk with your spouse and get on the same page. If one of you needs convincing, see "Tips for Getting a Skeptical Spouse on Board" in the back of the book.

☐ Choose a date to begin your detox. Ideally this will be a weekend or vacation day.

☐ Tell the kids. This is the hardest part of the detox. Flip back to page 52 for reminders for how to make this process as smooth as possible.

☐ Download your local library's app or talk with your librarian to learn how to take advantage of their hold system. Start putting great books on hold. It will take a few days before they are ready at your library branch. You want to start this process in time to have a stack ready to pick up by the time your detox begins.

☐ Loop in caregivers, babysitters, day-care workers.

☐ Write out your family's guiding principles from chapter 1. These are gravity points that help Mom and Dad sustain a long-term perspective throughout the detox.

☐ At some point toward the end of your detox, you will create your family's long-term plan. Have your parental antennas on high alert so you can begin to design that.

3

Notice Your Kids' Interests, Talents, Opportunities for Growth

SELAH WAS NINE YEARS OLD when we began our digital detox. Video games had been a favorite pastime since she was old enough to hold a remote control. It's not surprising that she protested our announcement at quitting screens. But after our detox and then a few more screenless months, her reaction completely transformed. She used much of her freed-up time to read anything she could get her hands on. At the end of our extended detox, her school tested her reading level. In a matter of a few months, Selah, who had always been a great student, had improved five grade levels in reading, from seventh grade to twelfth grade.

Proverbs 22:6 says, "Train up a child in the way he should go, even when he grows older he will not abandon it." Did you know "the way he should go" literally translates to "according to his way"?[1]

Our children are each wired differently, and our job as parents is to cultivate them according to those ways. On average, kids ages eight to eighteen are spending more than seven hours a day on a screen. If they are in school for seven hours, sleeping for nine, and on a screen for seven more, that leaves one measly hour for everything else: family dinner, exercise, errands, hobbies, reading. How can our kids possibly discover and hone their giftings when time doesn't allow for it?

The Notice part of your detox simply means that you are amping up your parental powers of perception. Study your child. Pay attention to what they love, what makes them tick, and even those areas that could use work. Take notes. Get to know them like never before.

I bet this part of the digital detox will easily be your favorite. There is nothing more gratifying than watching your children gravitate toward and practice their natural interests. Pre-detox, my oldest three kids would each cite a different video game as their favorite hobby. Post-detox? Each tends toward different *activities*: football, cooking, drawing, baseball, piano, teaching younger siblings to read. The screen break allowed us to get to know our kids better. I wasn't anticipating this, but it wound up being the best part.

Once screens were not an option, Jack would use an entire ream of paper to make his own comic books. He had always enjoyed drawing. But with time and brain space freed up during our detox, his creativity exploded. Graphic novels about super lizards and dog-men covered his desk. He asked for an opportunity to share his skills with the family by teaching a drawing class one night. I looked for books that assisted him in his interest, and it has fueled his talents. If your child has taken to comic book creation, grab a stack of blank notebooks and fresh pencils.

Caroline, four, has always adored dress-up, sparkles, and pink. After we removed passive screen watching from her days, she took to learning everything she can about makeup and beauty. Caroline watches carefully as I apply facial lotion, asking tons of questions. She plans imaginary parties and makes paper invitations to mail out to friends. Watching her gravitate toward what interests her has been immensely enjoyable as a parent. It also helps me understand how she is wired, which kinds of books and activities might interest her, and how I can connect with her in a way that she appreciates. We paint nails together and color pictures. I see a future aesthetician or CEO of a cosmetics company. The world is her oyster, and I have a better understanding of which opportunities will interest her as she grows.

Your digital detox will be like removing a filter. You will instantly see more clearly how your kids are uniquely made. Our own detox has been tremendously valuable in parenting five children as individuals, and in trying to identify how to love them well and cultivate their interests.

The proof is in the pudding

Kip and Mona Lisa Harding are two parents of average intelligence (their words) who raised ten kids of average intelligence (also their words). Each of their kids began college by age twelve. One became the youngest female doctor in the United States. Another child was an engineer. Several have become lawyers. All are bright and well-spoken.

Kip and Mona Lisa carefully observed how their young kids approached life. These parents studied their children's unique personalities and passions. Then they helped their kids uncover the path that aligns with the way each child is wired. They equipped each child according to their individual interests and skill sets, unleashing and then cultivating tremendous potential.

Their daughter Rosannah shared, "For most parents out there, when their eight-year-old says to them, 'I want to be an astronaut . . . when I grow up,' they smile and say, 'Oh, that's nice,' and go about their day. My dad, on the other hand, would take it to heart.

He would sign them up for the next Space Camp and introduce them to a friend of a friend who cleans rockets."[2] Rosannah had shown an interest in drawing at an early age. She went on to become the youngest member of the American Institute of Architects at age twenty-three.

Admittedly, not every parent wants their child entering college at twelve. But we can all agree that the Hardings have done something exceptional. They've unleashed their kids' unique passions and skills. This grew out of a very simple idea: studying your kids.

Too many of our parenting days are rushed. We are trying to "get through" the day, dropping on the couch, exhausted. So we send our kids to watch another show, play another game. It's time to take control. When your kids have moved out and you look back on your years of parenthood, what do you hope to see? You don't want to look back and see that you spent these short years merely "getting through." You want to have spent them well. You want to create lasting memories with your kids, teaching, training, investing in them. And in order to best invest in the people we love most, we need to get to know them better.

As parents, we are continually looking for ways to connect and grow closer to our kids as they get older. The most connected we have been as a family, the most clarity of purpose and drive we have experienced together happened as soon as we removed screens. It began the day we started our digital detox.

As a parent, you will gain intense clarity when you remove the screens that have been numbing out your kids.

Be on the lookout for potential giftings

Give your kids ample opportunities to make use of downtime without parental direction. Some kids might hit the ground running toward their favorite interests. Others might need a gentle nudge. Here are tips for creating spaces to identify talents and skills during their detox.

Get outside. Take a hike, a walk, a bike ride. Let your child give input on location and means of transportation if possible.

Is your child gravitating toward a bike every time? Learn about the different types of bikes—beach cruiser, ten-speed, unicycle—and share that information with your child. Teach him how to pump up a flat tire.

Does one child love hiking? Point out the features on your hike. Does one child stare at the wildflowers a little longer than the others? Find a book about wildflowers. Read it aloud together. Bring it on your hike. Let her explore. Show her how to press flowers.

Does another child stop to stare at bugs, fearless of creepy crawlers? Check out a book about insects from the library. Initiate a "bug hunt" in the backyard. Can you find an earwig outside? A ladybug? A butterfly?

Time spent outside is proven to reduce stress and improve cognition and sleep. Kids are missing opportunities each day to take advantage of this free and abundant resource.

Bake. No need to get fancy here, Gordon Ramsay. Boxed cake mix is all you need. Start small and see if your child is interested. Even very young kids—two-, three-, and four-year-olds—can help in the kitchen. Your smallest helpers can dump premeasured oil into the bowl or crack an egg. Older kids (eight or nine) can make recipes from start to finish after a little basic training. Our nine-year-old can bake chocolate chip cookies from scratch with a few assists from Mom.

Try this with your kids. Grab an apron and kids' cookbook and let them hone their skills. Assign them responsibilities like "snack maker," and give them options. Ants on a log? Crackers with cheese? Even a four-year-old can help prepare these foods. If one child is always lingering when you bake or cook, give him a few tools and a little freedom and watch what happens.

Assign presentations. Ask your children to become experts in a very specific topic of their choosing, and have them teach the family about it after dinner one night. Pay attention to the topics they choose. Three of our kids' most recent presentations spanned vastly different topics: How Google became Google, Cheetahs, and Chinese food. They are ten, nine, and seven. Younger children can easily contribute. Simplify the instructions. Read them a few picture books and ask if they want to share a fact they learned with the family. We love instilling a family culture that values continual learning about our beautiful, diverse world.

Create a talent show night. In the morning, tell your kids to think of a special talent they would like to share with the family that evening. Whatever they want. Watch their eyes grow in anticipation of their big moment. Watch as they scurry off to practice their talent. What does each child choose? What interests or talents are they clearly communicating to us when they can pick anything under the sun? In our home, we've seen singing, dancing, a weightlifting demonstration, a piano performance, a LEGO man dramatic production, and the reciting of a memorized poem or Bible verse. One time, our six-year-old little boy put a piece of paper on his stomach and ran fast enough to keep the paper from falling. Yep.

One teenage foster daughter sang beautifully for us during a family talent show. She vulnerably shared that her song selection ministered to her during trauma she had faced. We learned so much about this beautiful young lady in four minutes.

Our four-year-old conducted a seemingly random group-wide activity where we took turns banging on various toys and comparing the sounds. She beamed as she gave instructions and her older siblings followed them. As parents, we were able to observe how much this child loves to lead. That information helps us in knowing jobs we can give her around the home, extracurricular ideas, and even tips for her teacher when she is having a difficult day at school.

Sometimes kids simply need an invitation to express their creativity.

Be on the lookout for areas that need work

As you get to know anybody more closely, you start to see the good along with the not-so-good. This is just part of being fully known. It's a privilege to know anybody this closely, and one that parents are uniquely suited for, ordained as shepherds of their kids whether through birth or adoption. With screen diversions unavailable to your children, you will see with better clarity which natural personality traits you want to nurture in each child. Maybe you'll spot character traits that could use a little work. Fantastic! This is another golden opportunity to help equip your kids to be successful adults. If one child is prone to bossy, overly talkative, or lazy behavior, do not despair!

You are the caring adult entrusted with this worthwhile job. How do you proceed? Remember, kids are human beings. And all human beings have the capacity to be annoying sometimes. You get to be the person to meet your children's difficult personality traits with patience, unconditional love, and a long-view perspective. You are raising future adults. This is a tremendous opportunity to take inventory of your children and determine how to love and redirect them as individuals. You have the honor of coaching your kids as they grow into productive, kind, and responsible adults.

Josh Shipp proposes that your child's most annoying trait is their greatest strength in disguise.[3] Does your son recite baseball facts like a walking sports almanac? Maybe he'll be an ESPN host. Does your daughter talk your ear off about how she's budgeting her piggy bank contents? Maybe she'll host her own financial podcast. When a child has at least one caring adult in his life to redirect annoying behaviors and cultivate talent, he can soar to future success.

Here are ways to optimize your digital detox, putting your kids in situations to observe the areas where you can help them grow. **Assign a group chore.** Put one of your kids in charge of a group chore. Give each a turn at some point in your detox. Watch how each child leads, how they troubleshoot problems. One child might turn the cleanup into a game for the younger kids.

I overheard my oldest daughter leading her two younger sisters with this fun instruction: "All the toys on your floor are spy devices. We have to disarm them and return them to the toy bin!" Maybe a younger child will ask to play the cleanup song to motivate her siblings. Let them brainstorm ideas. You will be pleasantly surprised at their creativity.

You may run into a hurdle if your kids aren't used to bigger chores. Again, this is an opportunity to be a student of your kids. Remind them that in a household of however many people, that same number of people are responsible for contributing.

The chore should be simple enough for a small child to lead: empty the dishwasher as a team, pick up all the toys in the play room, clean up the kids' bathroom, collect all the stray shoes in the house and put them in the front closet.

Then observe what aspects of each child's leading style needs work. Do they give up quickly and need to grow in endurance? Do they grumble throughout the task? Do they get flustered easily when their siblings aren't listening? (I can relate to that!) There's an opportunity for a conversation about what to do when things don't go our way. These are lifelong skills, and we have the opportunity to assess and gauge where our kids need our help to develop them.

Play a board game. Even very young kids (two to five) can play simple games like memory matching, Chutes and Ladders, HiHo! Cherry-O. You might be surprised at your older kids' willingness to play these nostalgic games with younger siblings. Older kids (five and up) often enjoy playing Uno, Battleship, Sequence, Set, chess, and checkers.

Spend a few minutes covering game rules and expectations. It may require a lot of your patience and several reminders to get the game rolling. Every calm word you model for your kids during this time is invaluable. You're teaching them so much more than how to play a game. You're teaching them how to patiently wait their turn, how to be a gracious loser, how to tell the truth, how to appropriately value other people's feelings. We have ended many a board game session with tears and frustration. If that's you, it's okay! Keep going. What an opportunity to internally note each child's blind spots so we can gently and lovingly redirect them. They will get it, even if it takes some work.

Read aloud. Grab a few picture books and a blanket. Spread out on the lawn. Open a bag of chips and start reading. Vary your book genres and topics widely: biography, inspirational, fantasy, adventure, bestsellers. Read and watch your kids. Who sticks around longest? Who can't sit for beans? Who asks a zillion questions? Who can't get enough of Elephant and Piggie humor? Reading aloud to your kids is worthwhile on so many levels, and I'm excited to dive deeply into that in chapter 5. But for the purposes of observing your kids, reading aloud is a great venue to gauge their interests and ability to focus, share, ask thoughtful questions, and participate in conversation.

Maybe your four-year-old cannot sit quietly, for the love of Pete the Cat. How can your future kindergartner succeed if story time is such a challenge? Read-aloud time will prove an opportunity to troubleshoot now—what tools help him listen, focus, understand?

These ideas may require a small amount of up-front work on your end. But the investment will repay dividends. Take a few minutes to set your kids up with a chore or board game or outdoor activity. You are their training wheels to initiate problem-solving. An observant parent and a slight nudge can reveal a treasure trove of creativity waiting to burst out of your child's growing mind.

As parents, we are given the task and tremendous privilege of noticing our kids and observing their strengths and weaknesses. It's our job to steer them toward the right path, to equip them for life in the real world. We all want to raise well-adjusted kids who are kind and who know how to connect with other people, how to take turns, and how to express their needs in a considerate way. None of these skills come naturally. They must be developed and cultivated. We can probably all think of an adult who we wished honed these skills as a child. Maybe they work in your office. Maybe one of them is an extended family member. Let's give our kids the gift of a *present parent* as we coach, direct, and observe our children, measuring what they need from us to best grow into the adults they were made to be.

Let's watch them as they create, connect, and gravitate to their favorite activities—without the numbing effects of an electronic device.

You might be thinking, "What if my child is constantly bored and can't seem to think of his own ideas for playing independently? What if my kids are looking at me to entertain them?"

The next chapter will provide you with the tools you need.

DIGITAL DETOX CHECKLIST

Notice your child's strengths, interests, opportunities for growth

Look for hidden talents and interests

☐ Bake or cook: Which foods excite your child? Which cuisine is he or she drawn to?

☐ Presentations: What topics does your child continue to ponder? Animals? Medicine? Engineering?

☐ Talent show night: Name a talent that your child naturally possesses. Acting? Gymnastics? Soccer? Jewelry making?

Be on the lookout for areas that need work

☐ Group chore: Put away a load of laundry, sweep and mop the kitchen, empty the dishwasher. Pick something age appropriate. Let older children delegate. How is everyone at group projects? Grumpy? Bossy? Lazy? Make note of how you can create specific jobs to practice the traits that need work.

☐ Playing a board game: Celebrating winning, losing graciously, taking turns. Which areas of playing a board game are proving difficult for your child? With time and your patience, they can dramatically improve! Write down specific goals to improve.

☐ Read aloud: How are attitudes? How long are attention spans? (Be mindful of your expectations for what is age appropriate.)

Everyday opportunities for noticing

☐ Waiting: Can your child wait patiently for a doctor's appointment, for a package to arrive, for a sibling at practice?

☐ Sibling spats: Conflict resolution. What tools can you provide your child for navigating and resolving conflict?

☐ Frustration tolerance: What tools does your child need for negotiating frustration? Show them how you do this.

☐ Attention span: How long can your child participate in a conversation or listen to instruction? Try to grow this span little by little. Be patient.

☐ People skills: Does your child know how to converse with an adult? How to sustain a back-and-forth conversation? How to ask questions about the other person's life instead of monopolizing a conversation? (Many adults haven't mastered these skills! You're already ahead of the game if you are teaching them early!)

4

Develop a List of Screen-Free
Fun Together

The technology that promises to release us from boredom is actually making it worse. . . . The more you entertain children, the more
bored they will get.

ANDY CROUCH, *THE TECH-WISE FAMILY*

STEVE AND LAURA'S TWO-YEAR-OLD SON Ben was impulsive and difficult to parent. They struggled to keep him calm and
often relied on iPads and TV shows to keep him subdued. Their
four-year-old daughter had a calm, sweet disposition. Laura wondered how she could birth two kids who were so different from one
other. These exhausted parents wanted the days to pass as quickly
as possible. Whenever Ben threw a fit or became restless, his parents plopped him in front of the TV or handed him a phone. Steve
and Laura are good parents who love their son. They were working
with what they knew, and they assumed the screens were helping

because they appeared to calm Ben immediately. Plus, many of the apps and programs Ben used were advertised as "educational."

At the recommendation of Ben's pediatrician, Ben was assessed for speech delays, Autism spectrum disorder, ADHD, and a host of conditions. Every specialist agreed, Ben qualified for intensive therapies. Ben struggled to regulate himself for years. It was a long, slow road for the boy and his family. He grew and improved but struggled most days.

After reading about another family's successful digital detox, Steve and Laura removed every single screen from Ben's daily life when he was seven. They were shocked at what they found—a transformation in Ben that they had been praying for since he was two years old.

Within days, Ben was connecting emotionally and empathetically with his peers and with his family like never before. He began regulating his outbursts more quickly and more successfully. He began to troubleshoot his boredom and was bursting with creativity.

In retrospect, these parents believe that they'd been unwittingly numbing their young son on devices. They wish they had turned off the tablet sooner and instead spent those early years rolling up their sleeves and creating more spaces for toddler Ben to splash in the mud. Certainly, he was a difficult toddler in his own right. But entertaining him with screens did not allow him to grow and develop the way he could have.

Laura is convinced screens were the primary culprit in Ben's behavioral issues. Science supports her suspicions. One study showed that kids under the age of five who watched two hours of TV a day were 20 percent more likely to have attention problems at school age than kids who watched no TV. For every hour of television viewing, the risk of attention problems increases by 10 percent.[1]

Laura told me, "If I could go back in time, first I would give myself a big hug and say that I have what I need to parent Ben, even in his hardest days. I would encourage myself to handle his outbursts one at a time, without stressing about the future. I would tell myself to make a plan, a way to get him started on different activities that were simple and actually beneficial for his development. I wish I realized that we could have been working toward something better rather than desperately passing time. I wish I knew that screens were hurting and not helping his difficult behaviors."

There are many parents like Steve and Laura. Often they just need a plan, a list of specific and simple ideas to turn to—so screen entertainment doesn't seem like the only option when your own little Ben is standing in a puddle of maple syrup that he used to bathe the cat. Your list may not transform a problem child into a perfect child. But it will give you practical opportunities to know your kids better *while* helping their growth and development. Your list can assist you in creating redemptive moments amid your most difficult parenting days.

Parenting differently in a consumer-driven culture

Most of us would say that we want to raise thoughtful kids with strong characters. The best way to cultivate this is to put our kids in situations that require them to hone those skills. But too often, when we encounter a character problem or sibling conflict, we avoid it. When they get bored, we entertain our kids instead of parenting them.

We want to raise a future Ina Garten, but we prefer the speed and ease of Ronald McDonald. We don't want our kids to wind up overfed and underskilled, but sometimes our day-to-day parenting says otherwise. Let's change that. Let's parent today with the end in mind. Let's equip our kids and help pave the way for them to become strong, responsible, and emotionally healthy adults.

As we take a closer look at how our kids are wired, observing their interests and talents, we want to enable the best parts of them to shine. If your kids have been turning to video games, tablets, and TV for hours each day, you have been missing out on opportunities to study them. Now is the chance to change that. This will require some intentionality on your end, but it will be absolutely worth it.

Your digital detox will provide insight that Laura wished she had. That's why we are making a specific, tangible, and—most importantly—a FUN list of nonscreen activity options for your kids during the detox. There are several benefits to making a list:

Lists are clarifying. You, your spouse, and your kids will all have different ideas and passions for what goes on the list. When you sit together, grab the ideas floating around in your heads, and scribble them onto paper, they become tangible. You and the kids will all be on the same page—literally.

Maybe your son has been saving up for a new skateboard. As you make your list together, you get to see where your individual visions converge. Would you look at that? Dad wants yard workers and Billy's trying to save for a skateboard. Monetize some of the yard work, and everyone wins!

Lists are motivating. Brooklynn has always wanted to learn how to do a cartwheel. Add that to the list! When she practices and eventually masters the art of cartwheeling, Brooklynn will beam with a sense of accomplishment. Accomplishment motivates our kids to set more goals, and work toward them too.

Naming and listing a goal builds accountability. I always appreciate when my friends follow up with me to ask how I'm doing with a goal I set for myself. Our kids will appreciate the follow-up, even if they don't act like it in the short term. Work with your kids to set up a way to track their goals—like a calendar or their own detox journal. If you need something readymade, I have created a printable calendar you can post to your fridge, available on my website, www.mollydefrank.com.

Sweeten the deal for your kids with a celebration of their choosing at the end of your detox: ice cream outing, LEGO set of choice, miniature golf, trip to the movies together, whatever would excite your kids and fits the budget.

Lists make scary new endeavors feel more doable. Speaking of difficult endeavors, for a brief season in my life I had to give up all ice cream, cheese, and butter. (My infant son had a bad reaction if my milk contained dairy.) This food transition felt especially difficult because we were already on a vegetarian diet. No meat, *and* no dairy?! My mind continually paraded images of all the delicious foods I would no longer be able to enjoy. After a few days of wallowing in self-pity, I finally made a list of the foods I *could* eat. I wrote down meal after meal until I ran out of space on my paper. Suddenly, I didn't feel restricted; I felt excited about all the possibilities.

As your kids transition from screen-based leisure time to creativity-based leisure time, they might initially feel restricted and frustrated. That's okay! Because when you develop your list together, you will spell out countless individually tailored ways to have fun that have nothing at all to do with screens. You are creating a space for your kids to experience lightbulb moments.

Aside from the obvious benefit of the list in hand, your kids are going to experience intentional time with Mom and Dad, brainstorming solutions to a problem. How's that for growing responsible, relational, and thoughtful humans?

Boredom beckons creativity

Mom Sabrina shared a story with me that has become all too common. Sabrina and a few girlfriends rented a vacation home for a weekend. One of the moms brought her three-year-old son along for the trip.

The child began the weekend on the couch, iPad in hand, tapping away. After several hours, the battery died. Mom had forgotten to pack the charger. The little boy fell apart. He could not be consoled. His mother was obviously stressed out, and without options.

This child had not been taught how to entertain himself beyond the tablet. He had not practiced the art of troubleshooting his boredom by counting clouds or making dirt piles. He likely hadn't spent long periods of time in a waiting room with stacks of books. He was chronically overstimulated and now he was crashing.

I don't know this mother, and I am sure she loves her son deeply. She would never have intended to create a situation in which her child was unprepared to handle boredom. But without intentional planning, any parent can drift into this mistake.

There is a simple way out. We can teach our kids how to cope with setbacks and process boredom in real life, right now. This is the best way to prepare them for difficulty that will inevitably come.

Your kids will likely complain of being bored at the beginning of the detox. That's because screens offer pure entertainment without requiring much critical, deep, or imaginative thinking. The level of brain stimulation our kids receive on screens is enormous, while the mental and physical energy they expend is minimal. If they are coming off a standard American screen diet, the dopamine drop will be noticeable. The switch from "continually overstimulated" to "real life" might prove to be a rude awakening for some kids. We want to set them up for success as they reacclimate to life unplugged.

As parents, we too want to view boredom from a healthy perspective. Boredom is not a problem parents should solve for their kids. Boredom is an opportunity for our kids to invent, create, and use their brilliant minds. We do our children a great service if we develop that ability in them and start when they're tiny. Figuring out what to make of boredom is a sign of intellectual and psychological maturity. The exercise of being stuck in mental neutral, and then sifting through a list of potential duties and diversions, ranking them, and making a decision—this is a much-needed life skill. Let's get our kids practicing early.

The very concept of boredom is relatively new to humanity. The earliest citations of the word *bored* are from the mid-eighteenth century. Those citations also happen to be found in the correspondence of aristocrats and nobility.[2] They may not have had iPads, but they certainly did enjoy the kind of privilege that exempted them from manual labor.

Sounds like some kids you and I might know.

We want to equip our kids for life in the real world. Newsflash: Jobs can be boring. Folding laundry is boring. Sometimes school is boring. Jury duty is boring. Respectfully listening to an overtalker can be painfully boring. Part of learning to be a human being is finishing our responsibilities respectfully and with a good attitude, whether or not they are, in fact, boring.

Entertainment is not always a feasible solution to boredom here in the real world. Yet we are raising a generation of children who do not understand this concept, because we parents have not required them to.

We are parenting with the long game in mind. I know how it feels to see those other parents enjoying a quiet meal across the restaurant with all the children holding tablets, while yours are wiggling and talking a little too loudly. But take heart! Remind yourself that these years with kids under your roof are short, and you are in the process of laying a foundation for kind, thoughtful, and well-adjusted future adults. You are training them now for their future success. In a few years you will be wrinkled and gray, enjoying the early bird special, wishing for your wiggly kids back. We only raise our kids one time. We might as well do it right. Plus, as your kids switch their attention from screens to conversing, observing, reading, drawing, they will become less disruptive in public *and* more fun to be around.

This is another reason why creating a list of activities together is such a helpful and healthy exercise for our kids. We are asking them to think of what they enjoy, to consider the needs of others and the household, to look around at nature, and to spend some time in quiet thought. We are helping them use their minds and bodies to explore the world and discover all they are capable of.

Make the list

If we expect our kids to putz around the house and avoid video games, they are going to hate the detox. They will feel deprived and mopey, like everything fun is off-limits. (Like yours truly on a vegan diet.)

But . . .

If we can create an appealing alternative, then we can really begin to turn the tide, to make a shift—in their minds and in ours. And that course correction will change everything.

That's why we're making the list Laura wished she had. And the most important part of our list-making is you.

Mom's and Dad's attitudes are critically important to this process. I know you feel me on this. Mom and Dad set the tone of the home. There's a reason for the saying, "If mama ain't happy, ain't nobody happy." If Mom and Dad are in a bad mood, angry, frustrated, lacking confidence, pessimistic about success, the kids will soon follow.

Observe a case study of two list-making mothers.

Mildred: "Hurry up and sit down. What do you want to do since screens are banned? No more complaining about it, I'm sick of it. Let's GO, PEOPLE! Time for our list-making! Your dad and I have a date tonight, and I need to go shave my legs. They're hairier than a prairie goat!"

Yikes.

How about mom number two?

Kelly: "Guys! I made your favorite cookies so we can enjoy them while we write and color our Fun List. Come sit on this old blanket I laid out on the lawn. (Because it is my oldest blanket, I will not care if you spill chocolate on it, as it is no longer in use. I am a happy, kind mother.) Together we're going to brainstorm ideas for our detox. No idea is a bad idea. We will have a family list, and if you want to make your own individual list to keep separate, you are totally welcome to do that. I brought extra paper and pencils. My first idea was that we could create a sidewalk chalk village. I'm jotting that down as number one. Who else has an idea? Let's take turns. It can be anything."

Point is, wait until you are in a great mood. Or pull yourself together and fake it till you make it. But be cool, and no yelling. Grab a special treat. (You know who to ask if you need a recipe for vegan chocolate chip cookies.) Then gather your people and start that list! Shoot for at least fifteen ideas.

All you need to make your list:

a delicious snack

paper

pens, crayons, markers

most importantly, a mom and/or dad with a happy, optimistic attitude

Here are a few ideas to get you rolling if you need inspiration.

Ages 2 and up

Make a robot with household items destined for the trash. Toilet paper rolls, paper scraps, discarded cracker boxes cut up. Pour out a little glue on a paper plate. Surrender to the idea that a mess will be made. It will only take three minutes to clean it up afterward. Don't be uptight. Let the process happen.

Print customized coloring pages. Google "princess coloring page" or "R2D2 coloring page" or whatever your kid is into. One four-year-old I know requests very specific coloring pages. Like, "Princess holding her baby while driving a car and smelling flowers." (Never mind that this scene poses safety and legal problems.)

Let your kids make a general request, and then *you* choose the actual page to print because there are millions of search results and when the kids start trying to choose, that becomes its own problem.

Stuffed bear birthday party. Grab your child's favorite stuffed animals. Arrange them in a circle and bust out the granola bars or whatever snack you have handy. Sing "Happy Birthday." Have a dance party. Pretend the water is sparkling cider. You may need to get your little one started, imagining all of the fun. Let him or her help brainstorm and then let them lead.

Blanket fort. Show your children how to drape blankets or sheets, along with other general tips. Then tell them the best part is having your own secret hideout to look at books and get cozy. Read them a story inside, then leave a stack of board books as you go prep lunch.

Draw pictures or write letters for Grandma. If you can muster up the willingness to actually mail these pictures when your child is done, they will be motivated to do this regularly. I like to encourage my kids to color every part of the blank page, so that it's worth mailing. Any friend or relative is a great recipient of mailed preschooler drawings. Who doesn't like receiving envelopes of adorably disproportionate stick people?

Give them a large cardboard box and some markers. No further directions needed. What do they create? A spaceship? An elevator? A submarine? A castle? Sky's the limit.

Ages 6–10

Write a story or graphic novel. Invest in a few notebooks and journals. You can buy these for as little as a dollar, or you could get the leather-bound kind if you're fancy and if your children are not prone to destroying nice things. Some notebooks have preprinted comic book frames for your child to draw inside. My five- through twelve-year-old kids have spent hours writing stories and sequels. They are writing and spelling and illustrating. Their teachers would be so proud.

Build a LEGO city or scene. Help the kids imagine a scene they want to recreate in LEGO form. Or let them build a scene and then have the other kids guess what it is. Mom cooking dinner for dinosaurs? Legolas bossing around Orcs? An outer space pizza parlor? The possibilities are limitless.

Start a club. Sibling club. Butterfly fan club. Macarena dance club. Bird-watching club. Acting club. Painting club. Kids whose parents took away their screens club. (It's fine, they can process their feelings together while they brainstorm even more fun activities. I would suggest intervening if they try to unionize or picket dinner.)

Read. The best, most lasting gift of our detox was finding books that helped turn each of our kids into bookworms. This required a lot of work up front. But like the detox, it repaid huge dividends. If you want to incentivize reading before they actually love it, you could also have your kids track the books they've read via a sticker chart or their own handwritten list. A dollar store visit, special dessert, they choose dinner, or zoo trip if they read twenty books. Choose an incentive that fits your family and budget.

Set a goal to memorize a Bible verse, poem, the Gettysburg Address, states and capitals, all the presidents, a different language's alphabet . . . Among the most helpful parts of my elementary school experience was memorizing all of the prepositions and all the books of the Bible in order. I still sing the Bible books song in my head during church when the preacher tells us to flip to a specific book. Right now, our kids have incredible memories. Ask your kids which they'd be most excited to memorize. Or simply declare what you want them to memorize.

I am continually amazed at the amount of information our children can retain. If you have a few kids, let an older sibling teach a younger sibling a Bible verse. They can make up hand motions together. Ask them to surprise you when they have it committed to memory. And by all means, celebrate what they've accomplished with lots of verbal praise.

Ages 11–14

Become an expert, then teach us about a topic. Remind your kids that they are wired with unique talents and interests. Is your child a great speaker? Does she have a knack for explaining complicated information? For making great analogies? Affirm those talents! Then help her figure out what fascinates her. What does she stop to wonder about? Airplanes? The *Titanic* sinking? Mars? The history of the burrito? World hunger? The Bermuda Triangle? The Pittsburgh Steelers?

Check out books at the library on whatever topic your kids are even a little bit into. Let them peruse the children's nonfiction shelves. And then, by all means, *listen attentively* as they share what they've learned. Give them the floor at dinner for a few minutes. You don't want this to feel homework-y—more like they are sharing something that blew their mind, and they are sharing it with their favorite people. If what they share is new to you, let them know. How exhilarating for our kids to realize that their parents don't know everything, and that reading and a little legwork can open so many doors.

Have a friend over. Detox is a perfect time to invest in our kids' friendships face-to-face. Since Mom and Dad have taken away the phone, our poor kids will have to interact with one another IN REAL LIFE. The horror! But seriously, be flexible and accommodating if you can. Allow space and time for connection.

This is also a great opportunity to help your kids be intentional about the friends they choose. How many times have your kids encountered bullies or rude friends on social media or group chats? Think with them about which friendships are life-giving versus which are draining or downright damaging. Be mindful about

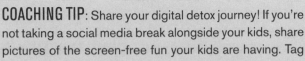

COACHING TIP: Share your digital detox journey! If you're not taking a social media break alongside your kids, share pictures of the screen-free fun your kids are having. Tag your posts #insteadofscreens and #DigitalDetox and discover inspiration from other parents on the same journey!

who you allow to speak into your kids' lives. Feed the friendships that are good, and create space for them to grow. Get the tea, the craft kit, the smoothie ingredients. Let your child bond with a good friend.

Bake. A box of Duncan Hines works fine. Teach your children to use the kitchen. Start them now, and by the time they get to college they will know how to make so much more than packaged ramen. If you aren't into sweets, let your children think of a recipient they might bless with their baking. The school secretary, a neighbor, a friend who is going through a tough time.

You can download one hundred additional free list ideas through my website, www.mollydefrank.com.

If you have kids in several of these age groups, direct an older child to lead the younger in one of the list items. Don't frame it as a chore, but as a joy and a responsibility. Part of being a loving and responsible human is caring for those littler than you. "Emma really looks up to you, Kate. You get to show her how eight-year-olds act, how they are helpers. You get to model what she wants to become when she is your age. Isn't that a cool role you have as her big sister?"

What if the list isn't working, and the kids are still complaining of boredom?

Get ready for a secret weapon that has worked literally 100 percent of the time I have used it on my children.

Child: "Mom, I'm bored."

Me: "Okay. You could go play outside, build a fort, write a letter, read a book. You could find something on the list we made together. Or if you are still bored, I have lots of laundry that needs putting away, and I would be so happy to have your help!"

Watch them scatter like cockroaches in the daylight. (The cutest and most lovable cockroaches, of course.)

We need not despair when our kids show us the parts of their personalities that could use improvement. If your next-door neighbor incessantly complained of boredom, you would politely exit, resigning yourself to the idea that some people are just that way. But when it's our young kids who are still learning everything about how to be a human, we can take heart. Parents enjoy a unique privilege—to shape, guide, and correct our favorite people.

When our children show us that they haven't yet learned a necessary skill or that they need some assistance, we can internally celebrate. Woo-hoo! Now we have clarity about what we can help them work through. If your child is having trouble getting started with nonscreen tasks, that's okay! Now you know how to come alongside and help.

Remember through it all that boredom is not a problem for you to solve.

Allowing our kids to be bored is really, really good for them. It invites them to create and invent. It's an opportunity to explore their giftings and interests, to learn more about the world and discover their place in it. What do your kids want to change in the world? What movements do they want to be a part of? What keeps them up and makes them tick? Rebekah Lyons says, "Your calling is where your talents and burdens collide."[3] Boredom helps our kids uncover and hone those talents, and to pay attention to the burdens quietly tugging on their hearts. Boredom nudges our kids into thoughtful reflection, where they can slow down to the speed of human thought and dwell in possibility.

The list you make with your kids is a bridge to help them go from screen-based to creativity-based play. They might use your list daily. You might use it to remind them not to complain of boredom, lest they wind up polishing baseboards.

When all is said and done, by the end of a successful detox, don't be surprised if your kids no longer consult the list. Knowing the list is standing by for consultation is the best part of making it. Like a blankie for your boredom. You don't really need it. But sometimes it makes them feel comfier. You might find that the exercise of brainstorming was enough to show them that they have everything they need to troubleshoot and problem-solve on their own.

Boom. Now they have learned a great life skill.

─── 5 ───

Open the Books!

The man who does not read has no advantage over the man who cannot read.

UNKNOWN

AS YOU EMBARK ON YOUR DETOX, you are probably nervous. You might be thinking, *What in the world will my kids do with all of their spare time? Are they going to complain of boredom for two weeks straight?* Don't worry. You won't be left hanging. We already have our handy-dandy list to fall back on.

And now we are going to discuss replacing much of their newly vacant time with something productive, fun, and beneficial.

Books!

Were you hoping for something more exciting? If so, please indulge me for a moment while I persuade you that books are not boring. They are in fact a secret portal to uncharted worlds. Your very own wardrobe—with or without the lion and witch—that happens to fit in your hands.

Jim Trelease suggested that if someone were to invent a vitamin that offered the following benefits, parents would line up for miles to get their hands on it. Imagine a vitamin that was proven to provide the following benefits:

- Taking this vitamin is the single most important way to build knowledge for future success in reading.[1]
- Kids who take this vitamin score half a year's schooling higher on standard tests.[2]
- This vitamin is more effective than private education or expensive tutoring.[3]
- Kids who take this vitamin read the best, no matter their family's income level.[4]
- After one year of taking this vitamin every day, kids improved their reading levels, sometimes by nearly four grade levels.[5]
- After taking this vitamin, struggling young readers measurably increased their reading abilities. (Brain scans confirmed these children literally created new connections, rewiring their brains.)[6]

What if I also told you that this vitamin is free? It is naturally occurring, and there are zero side effects. Oh, and your neighborhood has a free dispensary. Also, it's legal, and not just in California.

What is this magic vitamin?

Reading.

Reading requires practice, as with any learned skill. Like baseball or piano, the more you do it, the better you become. And the less you practice, the wonkier you will be. And yet the majority of our kids are not reading for pleasure. They are not developing this free skill that will change the trajectory of their future.

"My kids spend all day at school. I don't want to tack on more work!"

We are not talking about book reports. We are talking about the kind of reading that transports you to another time and place, the kind that you do for *pleasure*. The books that you wonder about in between reading sessions. The ones you can't wait to discuss with your book club. The kind of reading that changes your life. Have you ever read a book that spoke to your heart in a way that a TV show simply could not? We are giving our kids a lifetime gift when we cultivate a love for reading. The earlier the better.

Hook them on reading *because* it's pleasurable. But a lovely and sneaky thing happens along the way. They learn deep thinking, delayed gratification, empathy. Sure, tweens sometimes "read" when they are on a screen, but they are most often reading randomized snippets of information: tweets, snap captions, an inch-deep and mile-wide digital dumpster. When our big kids are staring at screens, they are not deep-reading, thinking critically, practicing the skills necessary to build their brains. Encouraging them to read for pleasure turns out to be both enjoyable and educationally enriching.

When we mentally segment our kids' educational time, assuming that their learning happens during school and their leisure happens at home, we miss out on an enormous window of opportunity. By the end of eighth grade, a child has spent 9,000 hours in school, compared with 95,000 hours outside school. If our kids are not reaching their potential in reading, we can hardly blame the teachers.

Teachers fill their instructional hours with what the state mandates them to teach. There is only so much time in the school day. Parents, on the other hand, have the freedom to introduce enriching learning experiences in a fun way. Kindling a love of reading starts at home. What an incredible opportunity parents have to instill passion for a skill with innumerable benefits, *and* which happens to be tremendously enjoyable!

"But my child doesn't like to read."

This, my friend, is not a thing. I say this sympathetically but also confidently, as a fellow parent who spent many years believing the same thing. **A child who doesn't enjoy books is a child who has not yet met his genre.** Your mission is to play matchmaker. You are going to help your child discover the books that will light up his world. Using your observations about interests and skill sets, you will find this step a fun and gratifying challenge. And I'm here beside you to help. I brought great book recommendations too.

If you are still skeptical about your child embracing the world of books, below you will find a handy-dandy quiz.

My child enjoys (check all that apply) . . .

☐ cooking	☐ sculpting
☐ food	☐ painting
☐ dinosaurs	☐ drawing
☐ nature	☐ origami
☐ insects	☐ LEGO
☐ stories	☐ jokes
☐ birds	☐ riddles
☐ learning a new, impressive skill (skateboard, magic tricks, gardening, guitar, pool)	☐ facts
	☐ action
	☐ comics
☐ thinking	☐ sports
☐ being persuaded	☐ politics
☐ the *Titanic*	☐ faith
☐ NASCAR	☐ cars
☐ piano	☐ trains
☐ drums	☐ laughing
	☐ crying

If you checked one or more of the above items, congratulations! Your child is a perfect candidate to become a bookworm. If you were unable to check any of the boxes above, I hate to be the person to tell you this, but your "child" is actually protozoa. The good news is that protozoa are even easier to digitally detox than children!

In the absence of the continuous digital-dopamine release loop, you are retraining your kids' brains to find pleasure in the world around them. Detox mode is the perfect time to rekindle a love of reading because the slower, sustained dopamine release of a good book doesn't have to compete with the steroidal dopamine release your kids get while playing MEGA ZOMBIE ATTACK BUSTERS video game, or whatever.

A huge part of our job as parents is to inform our kids' desires as they grow. One of my babies would crawl around the yard, picking up every single object in her path. She would promptly deposit the object into her mouth, chew it, then spit it out or eat it, depending on her satisfaction level. Sometimes, the object would be a stray Cheerio. Other times, the object would be much, much worse. It took time and training, and many instances of my running toward her yelling, "NO! Spit it out!" to educate this little love that just because it's there, doesn't mean you should eat it. Duh, for the rest of us. But for a newb like her, this was part of learning how the world works. As her parent, my job was to educate her desire for healthy food that is also clean and tastes good and comes on a plate, without dirt on it. (We are very fancy people with high standards.)

My ten-year-old read *Love Does* by Bob Goff as I spent several days wrapped up in a major educational setback for a different child. That book ministered to her heart in ways that I could not have during that time. After she was done, we bonded over Goff's zest for life and commitment to his faith. You may not share my faith. But I know you have things you want to impart on your kids before they move out. We would all do well to number the days of our kids' lives in our homes and ask, "What do I want to share?

What do we want to cover while they are still under my roof? Which books changed me? Which wrecked me in a way I can't describe?"

Books, it turns out, are a monumentally simple and enjoyable way to impart wisdom and teaching to our children.

"Okay, let's try it. Where do I start?"

Start with a stack of books. You can buy the books, of course. But once your little reader gains momentum and consumes several books per week, you will need to decide between the book budget and the grocery budget. This is why your local library is about to become your BFF.

Here's a little secret that you probably already know. Not all books are worth your time. There, I said it. Some books are boring. Some are poorly written. Others don't have great messaging. I do not happen to agree with folks who want kids reading, no matter the message. There are millions of books available to read, but not all of them are worthy of our time and attention.

As we select books for our kids, we will do so intentionally. This does become more difficult as the kids get older, but we are still going to do our best. Older kids will have had a few years to grow in wisdom and discernment. We will help them select books but also want them to develop the skill of discernment. *Should I be reading this one about the murderous prom queen?* your fifth grader wonders. (That'd be a no, sweetie.) But we do want them getting into the practice of using their own developing sense of wisdom to make good choices. Our library book stacks will teach our kids to desire books in the first place, while helping inform which *types* of books they should desire.

These book suggestions are like that: clean, good, nourishing. Each has been selected because it made us laugh, cry, or think. Some titles did all three. Start reserving these books and then we will discuss your library outings themselves. Many public library systems have their own apps. Download and connect it to your library card. Then you can begin to place books on hold as you come across new recommendations.

Here are a few book recommendations to get you going.

Picture books

Read them aloud and have fun with them (as in, don't rush and don't act like a curmudgeon), and you might find that your independent readers will continue to pick up the books and reread to themselves or to a younger sibling. Double win!

Rosie Revere, Engineer by Andrea Beaty

Halfway Herbert by Francis Chan

Hair Love by Matthew A. Cherry

The Story of Ruby Bridges by Robert Coles

Miss Rumphius by Barbara Cooney

Mercy Watson books by Kate DiCamillo

The Gruffalo by Julia Donaldson

The Snail and the Whale by Julia Donaldson

The Seven Silly Eaters by Mary Ann Hoberman

Everything You Need for a Treehouse by Carter Higgins

A Mother for Choco by Keiko Kasza

The Jesus Storybook Bible by Sally Lloyd-Jones

You Are Special by Max Lucado

Roxaboxen by Alice McLerran

Who Wet My Pants? by Bob Shea

Press Here by Hervé Tullet

If I Built series by Chris Van Dusen

Elephant and Piggie books by Mo Willems

Bear Snores On by Karma Wilson

The Napping House by Audrey Wood

Read aloud

My Father's Dragon by Ruth Stiles Gannett

I'm Just No Good at Rhyming and Other Nonsense for Mischievous Kids and Immature Grown-ups by Chris Harris

Winnie-the-Pooh (the original) by A. A. Milne

Amelia Bedelia by Peggy Parish

Where the Sidewalk Ends by Shel Silverstein

Independent readers for ages six and up

The Miraculous Journey of Edward Tulane by Kate DiCamillo

The Adventures of Sophie Mouse series by Poppy Green

Magic Tree House series by Mary Pope Osborne

Junie B. Jones series by Barbara Park

Geronimo Stilton books by Geronimo Stilton

Thea Stilton books by Thea Stilton

Read alone or read aloud for ages nine and up

One of our favorite reads for older kids is *A Long Walk to Water* by Linda Sue Park. Check out my website for updated lists of book recommendations for older and younger kids. As your kids get older, they will be reading books faster than you can vet them. Help your kids learn to select and sift their own books.

Selecting books for teens and tweens

I learned a great tip from Sarah Mackenzie, founder of the *Read-Aloud Revival* podcast: "Young adult" is a book *genre*, not a *reading level*.[7] The young adult genre is aimed at tweens and teens, and themes often revolve around pushing boundaries. Some books within this genre expose kids to racier and sexually charged topics that parents may not feel comfortable with. What parent has the time to vet a two-hundred-plus-page book for each of her middle graders? Often parents shrug and say, "Hey, at least they're reading." But you don't have to resign yourself to this.

Mackenzie's observation lifted a huge weight off my shoulders as a parent. We live in a magnificent world with millions of different books. So remind your children that when Mom or Dad limits certain titles, there are still *millions* remaining. With a little bit of intentionality, you can provide more great books for your children than they could possibly read through.

Guide your kids toward tried-and-true options by providing many preselected titles. Continue to come alongside them as they develop the skill of choosing great books for themselves. Of course, they should play a part in selecting their own books. But preselecting books from which they choose is wise. (In the same way that you would not allow your young child to watch a rated-R or NC-17 movie, you preselect some parent-approved options and let them choose from among them.)

Mom Caitlin hit a wall trying to find books for her thirteen-year-old son during their detox. Hayden wasn't interested in the first few tween-genred books she had helped him select. She pointed to their family bookshelf. "How about *Rich in Love?*"

A nonfiction book written by a longtime foster family sat on their shelf. The book chronicles Irene and Domingo Garcia's life as a young married couple wrought with problems. It is full of real-life trials, mistakes, and abuse. The Garcias share how God redeems broken situations and uses ordinary people to care for orphans.

It was written for adults. But Hayden is a strong reader, and his parents wanted to show him how God responds to real-life hardship, and how he even uses tragedy to bring about good. Hayden is also the oldest child in a family that had fostered and adopted two children. He was intrigued. "Might as well give it a shot," he said. With video games off the table, he didn't have his go-to options during downtime. Hayden finished *Rich in Love* in a few days. He couldn't put it down.

There are so many books available for us and for our kids to read, it can sometimes feel overwhelming. But it's also encouraging, because when it comes to matchmaking books and kids, if at first you don't succeed, try, try again. And ask your friends! Ask people whose values are similar to yours.

If you would like a more comprehensive list of our family's favorite books for readers of all ages, you can download a free list on my website, www.mollydefrank.com. If you are looking for additional curated booklists, I always find great ones are created by homeschooling parents and teachers.

So now you have specific book titles to get you started. Place a few of the previously mentioned books on hold at your local library. You will find many that keep your children turning the pages.

"Got any tips for finding great books on our own?"

Over time, you will begin to identify specific authors and illustrators your kids love. As your kids get to know their favorites, search for more books by those people, and then place those on hold through your computer or smartphone app.

Another helpful tip: Search Amazon for a favorite book your kids already know and love. Scroll allllll the way down to the bottom of the page, *past* the sponsored books, past the customer reviews, and you will find an area that says, "Customers who viewed this item also viewed . . ." Here you will find an entire lineup of similar books, all of which will display a rating. Go back to your library app and place a hold on all the titles that catch your interest, or books you think might interest your child. (And you can point out to your kids that these are excellent examples of technology being used to serve your family well!)

In addition to being a treasure trove of books, your library is also a resource for book*lists*. The American Library Association awards all kinds of accolades after sifting through piles of books. It's basically like the Academy Awards, but for books.

For example, the Caldecott Medal is awarded to outstanding picture books. Simply search for Caldecott Medal recipients and finalists, and you'll easily find a list of every winner since 1938. Boom, now you have eighty-plus titles to check out and enjoy. If your child gravitates toward beautiful pictures and illustrations, place those titles on hold, stat.

For your beginning reader, check out the Geisel Award recipients. This is another award by the American Library Association.

Your chapter book readers might enjoy selections from the Newbery Medal award recipient list, which recognizes excellence in children's literature.

Several of my children have been thrilled with nearly every award winner we've picked up. But not all of them. Just because a group of librarians agree that a book is excellent doesn't mean that every distractable, Fortnite-withdrawing eight-year-old will be riveted by it. Academy Award–winning films are sometimes quirky, artsy, and esoteric. Meanwhile, the Spiderman movies thrill the masses. Books can be the same way.

"Got any tips for kids who don't want to read?"

Some kids' eyes roll into the backs of their brains when Dad or Mom attempts to sell them on the magical world of books. If that's the boat you're in, take heart! There is still hope.

My most reluctant reader required more attention from me than simply Googling a booklist. At seven, he didn't like reading for fun. That was that. Or so I thought, until we began our digital detox. My nine-year-old daughter was devouring books at an accelerated rate thanks to our screenless season. But my bouncy boy? Not so much. I realized that if we could only ignite his love of reading, he would fill his time with a productive, pleasurable, and educationally enriching activity. But how did we get him to switch from nonreader to book lover? We went to the library.

He enjoyed the library from day one, flipping through various titles. But he never "happened upon" a book that grabbed him. It took a few hours and book-matchmaking trial and error, but that kid *finally* began to discover genres he loved. I searched the stacks, checking out copies from the Super Chicken Nugget Boy, Hardy Boys, I Survived . . . (historical fiction), and Geronimo Stilton series. I sat down and showed each one to my son. Without the video games beckoning him, he took a little extra time to flip the pages. He tolerated a few of them. But once he began reading Geronimo Stilton, something clicked. The kid likes fantasy. Who knew? He also happens to be a sucker for strange-but-true fact books. Put a graphic novel in his hands today, and he will retreat to his tiny reading closet, from whence he will only be lured out via chocolate chip cookies or upon finishing the book in his hand.

If you had told me three years ago that I would need to remind this specific child to close the books while his friends are over for a playdate, I would have patted you on the head and checked your vitals. Yet here we are. Your detox is the ideal zone to stir up your kids' inner book lover. It all starts at the library.

"I'm supposed to take all my noisy, wild kids to the library?"

I know firsthand that shepherding loud, grabby toddlers through a quiet place is enough to give you the sweats. Might as well be guiding blind feral cats through a museum, right? But the episodic chaos is worth the long-term gain. You are teaching your small kids how to behave in a quiet place—without a screen to entertain them. This from a mother who has more disastrous library stories than pages in this book to describe.

But guess what? Someone has to teach our precious children about the basic norms of the civilized world. And that someone is you.

That's why taking the kids to the library is not a burden—or at least, not *only* a burden. It's also an opportunity to teach your favorite little people about the delightful world of books. If your children are small, or if you have a lot of them, it will be hard. Do it anyway. Your kids will learn and grow with every visit. Will they fail and scream and embarrass you? Absolutely. (I'm talking about the toddlers here, but no judgment if these words also apply to your teenager.) Keep going. You are normalizing library visits. You are also encouraging them to develop responsibility.

Resist the simplicity of checking out all your family's books on one account. Watch your kids light up as they scan their very own cards with their names on them. They are responsible for taking care of and returning their library books. Put your four-year-old in charge of a board book. Tell her that the library is a special place where we share great stories with all the people in our big city! But part of caring for everyone in our city is taking great care of the books we share together. Can she take special care of this book while she borrows it for the next two weeks? This is her big girl job. She can do it! (Between you and me, plan for a little bit of failure along the way, but look for opportunities to point out and celebrate growth!)

Many libraries have arrangements with local restaurants that offer incentives for kids who read a certain number of books. Once they reach their goal, they get a certificate that can be redeemed for a free book or personal pizza or whatever. Look out for these programs as you head in. They help sweeten the deal for reluctant readers. Our library also hosts story times, LEGO building competitions, teen and adult book clubs, free concerts, and crafts. Take advantage of this resource!

Your library visits are so much more than a quick stop for a stack of books. You are teaching your tiniest kids that the nonfiction section is not an obstacle course, how to wait their turn quietly, and how to respect and return borrowed items. Expect hiccups. But the more you visit, the more your kids will begin to understand the way it all works. Create a recurring library day: Tuesdays after school, Thursdays after work, or build it into the weekend—Saturday morning books and donuts. Make it fun.

And as you press through the hard, embarrassing parts, you might be pleasantly surprised to see your kids come out on the other end, book in hand. Soon your feral cats will be well-behaved bookworms, begging you for another trip to the library.

6

Reading Aloud: The Magic Ticket

When she was hardly more than a girl, Miss Minnie had gone away to a teacher's college and prepared herself to teach by learning many cunning methods that she never afterward used. For Miss Minnie loved children and she loved books, and she taught merely by introducing the one to the other.

WENDELL BERRY, *WATCH WITH ME*

SOMETIMES PARENTS ARE SO CLOSE to utter transformation, just on the verge of hooking their reluctant readers into the magical world of books. The missing link between a child's book aversion and book affection is as simple as a parent reading aloud. Seriously. Think back to your own elementary school experience. Remember when your teacher would read a book aloud after lunch? You'd rest your sweaty face on your desk while the A/C did its thang. Ten minutes later, the teacher's voice would slow down, signifying a chapter's end. *No!* you'd think. *You can't leave it here! I'm enraptured. I need more!* You can make those kinds of memories and build that same anticipation and love of story in your living room. Huge bonus: Read-aloud time is often the bridge between a reluctant reader and a bookworm.

Open a book and plop a kid on your lap (assuming yours is, in fact, a lap-sized child; don't be weird). And then? Read aloud, my friend. Make it fun. Give your characters accents. Read a few pages, ten minutes, or even an hour. Set a minimum, maybe five minutes. You can reassure your reluctant newbie that we are doing this thing for five minutes, and if we want to keep going, we can. But if we'd like to be all done for today, that's all right too. Check in after five minutes. "Want to be all done, or should we keep going?"

Read for however long you and the kids can handle. Just read aloud. This is a game-changing parenting hack for kids of all ages. I exaggerate not. Reading aloud to your kids is the simplest and most effective activity for bonding, stress relief, education, listening comprehension, vocabulary building, team building, imagination spurring, building sustained attention, and more. Research supports it. Intuition insists on it. Even when the chaos ensues (and chaos will occasionally ensue), reading aloud is worth your time. It will repay itself one thousand times over in emotional, relational, and intellectual dividends. And for proof? I offer you a story.

"Grab a snack and come to the lawn for read-aloud time!" I announced to my six children. The sink was piled high with dishes. Laundry needed folding. But the chores could wait. I knew we all needed some bonding and Bible time. Frankly, I needed the morale boost. I hoped this pocket of read-aloud time would refresh all of us. I prepared for an idyllic scene of sibling bonding and spiritual growth.

"Can you grab the storybook Bible from the back seat of the car?" I asked my four-year-old. She ran off to look for it while the rest of us waited. Five minutes and three irrational sibling fights later, my book-fetcher returned empty-handed.

"I couldn't find it," she said, wearing an old pair of sunglasses and *multiple* baseball hats. She had clearly spent the time excavating crevices in the car. I stomped off to find the Bible myself. It was exactly where I said it was.

I was miffed, but committed to seeing this read-aloud time through. I returned to the lawn and began to read. "'One day, Jesus was—'"

"OUCH! He hit me! Mom!!!"

"Seriously? There is an entire lawn to sit on. Spread out. Use double-arms distance and common sense. Let's go, people. . . . Okay. . . . 'One day, Jesus was—'"

"Mom, can you pause? I want to refill my snack."

"No. 'One day, Jesus was—'"

"STOP LOOKING AT ME!" A ridiculous argument broke out. It also broke the final straw of my rapidly fraying patience.

"I'm done. This has been a monumental waste of my time," I huffed. Tossing the children's Bible on my chair, I retreated back into the house, seeking solace in my sink full of dishes. Not my best mothering. But I was frustrated, darn it! I wondered if they were absorbing any of the reading, the stories, the lessons and love I had been pouring out. I thought they had been enjoying our regular read alouds, but the disruptions were making me question everything. Why must they act like brawling fraternity brothers? How could they absorb even a smidgen of my beautiful stories when they're arguing and distracted? It seemed like every time we read aloud together, there was always an obstacle. What was the point?

I scrubbed the dishes and wiped down the counters with just the right combo of elbow grease and mom guilt. I called the kids back inside so we could put away laundry together. Two of the boys, seven and nine, picked up an old argument. I opened my mouth to intervene. But before I could say a word, my four-year-old foster daughter ran in between her big brothers, holding up a hand toward each of them. She wielded the confidence and authority of a principal at a continuation high school. "Stop!" she proclaimed. The boys froze in surprised confusion.

"Is this what you want?" she went on. "To repay evil for evil? Like those brothers that killed the other one because of the fruit-present to God?" Cain and Abel. We'd read that story a week or two ago. Not only had she understood and remembered it, but now she was using it to exhort her older siblings. This four-year-old child was calling her big brothers to repent!

She kept going. "Look at him!" she motioned each brother to the other. "He is your BROTHER. You need to LOVE each other. God wants you to love each other." She sat back down and resumed her laundry pile, shaking her head. I turned to my ten-year-old daughter; both of our jaws had dropped. The boys' fight was silenced. We all paused for a few seconds to process what had just happened, and then the giggles began. The three older kids, including the two who had been fighting, were shocked. What wisdom, what clarity and commanding presence—from a four-year-old! My pint-sized prophetess hid a proud smile as she realized that she had completely transformed the mood of the room.

Our read-aloud times mattered. All of them mattered. And so do yours. Each time you sit and read aloud to your tiny humans, your words are planting seeds in the minds and hearts of the people you love most. Yes, one kid will inevitably be doing headstands while another dribbles chocolate milk down his brand-new shirt. . . . But guess what? They are gleaning a LOT from the time you have taken to lay out that blanket and simply, patiently read the words on the page.

While you read aloud the story of Abraham and Isaac from the incomparable *Jesus Storybook Bible*, you can't possibly know what each of your kids is thinking. One child is wondering if that nearby squirrel minds eating acorns without ketchup. But another is suddenly struck by the depths of God's sacrificial love for him. We never know the exact moment our children's hearts and minds are receptive to the teaching we attempt to impart. That's why we impart it often, focusing on our own calling to shepherd our kids with a long-game view.

The superhero in plain sight: Dad

While mothers read to their kids more often than fathers, research shows that it's the *father's* reading aloud that more significantly predicts a child's reading comprehension and language skills.[1] This is huge. Moms typically spend more time with their kids than dads, but the impact of a dad reading aloud to his kids has proven to be heftier. Dads, don't squander a massive opportunity to bolster your kids' brains. You have so much to offer your little and big ones. Reading aloud is simple, nearly effortless, and tremendously enjoyable for you and your kids. Watch your wife beam at you as you take ten minutes a day to crack open a book and simply lend it your voice. (Her beaming might be 50 percent due to the precious sight, 50 percent because you've given her a well-deserved break. But who cares? Happy wife, happy life!)

Another study showed that when dads read for pleasure, their sons read more. The sons of reading dads also have higher test scores.[2] Even reading quietly *to yourself* positively impacts your kids. They are watching you because they think you're awesome. If you think reading is cool, they think it's cool.

For a deeper dive into the incredible impact dads have on their kids' literacy and learning, check out *Jim Trelease's Read-Aloud Handbook*, chapter 5, "The Importance of Dads."[3]

"Can we stop reading aloud once the kids can read themselves?"

During our digital detox, one major rhythm to change in our house was the frequency of read-aloud sessions. I learned more about the practical and scientific benefits of reading aloud, including the fact that there are virtually zero drawbacks. (Maybe a little bit of inconvenience and frustration on my end, but that's par for parenting anyway, right?) Reading aloud is a critical component of life for our youngest kids. Author Mem Fox says that kids need to hear a thousand stories read aloud before they begin to learn to read for themselves. That might sound daunting, but she also points out that three stories a day will deliver one thousand stories in a year alone.[4] And parents are blessed to have five full years with our littles before they reach school. We can totally do this.

The benefits of reading aloud are not relegated to preschoolers. In fact, experts argue that some of the most dramatic benefits of reading aloud are observed in older children. One failing Boston school was brought back from the brink of shutdown in 1984, after a new principal took the reins and immediately adopted a simple but transformative change. Thomas P. O'Neill Jr. implemented ten minutes of read-aloud time every morning, and ten minutes of quiet time for pleasure reading at the end of every school day. O'Neill was onto something, and the proof was in the pudding. After one year, test scores climbed. After two years, student enrollment was up. Three years later, the school had the highest reading scores in the city of Boston, and there was a fifteen-page waiting list of children who wished to attend.[5]

With screens off the table during your detox, your kids are going to have a lot more free time. You are like their tour guide. "Welcome to earth, my younglings. You are new here, whereas I have been around the block. I am excited to show you all of the things: books, the outdoors, games, sports, and friendships waiting to blossom." Your kids are going to learn about the world through their direct experiences or through the stories of others who have gone before. You may not be able to fly your herd to Japan, take an African safari, or go on a Hawaiian vacation. Time-travel machines are difficult to come by these days, due to the small detail of their not having been invented yet. But! When you read a great story aloud together, you have practically reaped the benefits of both time travel and even telepathy. You can learn from the brains of the smartest astrophysicists or be entertained by the most masterful storytellers. And you get to do this from the comfort of your own lawn or huddled under blankets in front of the fireplace.

But our kids won't view reading like this unless someone shows them.

That someone is you. And the journey is a joy to behold. Buckle up.

"I'm too busy to replace all my kids' screen time with reading aloud to them."

I'm talking ten minutes of reading aloud per day, as many days as you can in a week. Another perk of reading aloud to your kids is that it jump-starts their interest in solo reading. Your detox period is the perfect time to create book lovers in your home, because they don't have a digital dopamine box beckoning their stunted attention spans. Your parental nudges and book supply will get them started. With a little up-front work, by the time the detox is over, their interest in reading will have been sparked. Keep feeding them more books. Nudge, nudge, nudge. This has worked for every child who has lived in our home. Parents I've helped through a detox have testified to the same results. If you increase book supply and nix the easy distractions, they will read. And I'm not only talking about kids who *can* read. Pre-readers *love* books! Toddlers can devour books, sometimes even literally. This is why I recommend board books for your littlest and most destructive literary connoisseurs.

The pockets of time when you used to rely on a screen to occupy your children? Soon you will be able to use books instead. I kid you not. Waiting at a restaurant? Books. Doctor's waiting rooms? Books. Need the kids who are post-napping age to hang in their room for fifteen minutes while you take an important phone call? Books.

Of course, you likely can't do a straight exchange from iPad to book. You need to do a little parental investing. But it will require less of that than you think. And your time spent will create cherished family memories.

My daughter was seven when I handed her *The Magician's Nephew*, from C. S. Lewis's Chronicles of Narnia series. She read a few pages and then told me the language was strange and difficult to understand. I sat with her and read a few pages aloud. Once she no longer had to work to sound out and grasp older British phrasing, she could focus on the story. Once she was hooked on the story, she asked to have the book back. The pleasure she experienced from the story itself motivated her to work a little harder to sound out words and wrestle with unfamiliar phrases. She finished that book all by herself, after a little bit of time with Mom and a few questions about unfamiliar phrases.

Reading aloud places you beside your child, in her zone of proximal development. This is the space between where she is currently and where she can grow. As a parent, you get to coach and encourage your child to stretch from her current level toward her potential. Good parents already do this—teaching a crawler to walk, teaching a wobbly armed rookie how to play catch, teaching a miniature pianist to practice through a difficult piece. We simply apply this same principle to reading. If your son says he doesn't like to read at all, grab a graphic novel like *The Action Bible* or *Mighty Jack*. Sit beside him for a few pages, or even an entire book. Ask him if he wants to finish the story on his own or for you to read it aloud.

Watch the magic happen.

"Okay, we are in. Remind me of the benefits so I don't lose heart when it gets hard sometimes."

Here are a few major benefits of reading aloud as a family:

Sibling bonding. As read-aloud maven Sarah Mackenzie points out, when you read to your kids, they are rooting for the same characters, laughing at the same jokes, creating a shared culture in the home—together.[6] One moment your kids are at each other's throats. The next, they are sipping hot chocolate, jointly hoping that Bilbo can escape the fiery wrath of Smaug.

Instilling a desire to read individually. Your child's listening comprehension is higher than his reading comprehension. A kindergartner is an emerging reader. It might take him twenty minutes to slowly and painfully sound out each of the fifteen tiny words in his Bob Book. But that same child can audibly understand a fourth-grade reading level. If Mom or Dad snuggles up on the couch to read *Because of Winn-Dixie*, that kindergartner begins to appreciate more complex stories, builds his vocabulary, and anticipates the fruit of his reading labor. *If I keep learning*, he thinks, *I will be able to read longer books like this soon!*

Cultivating the ability to sustain attention. Sustained attention does not come naturally to anybody. (For reference, please see a two-year-old.) All humans must practice and learn the ability to concentrate. That's because these systems in the brain are not developed yet in young kids. Developing the skill of focused attention and concentration takes years. For that reason, the attention of our youngest kids is ready for the taking. We parents know exactly what has been taking this attentional opportunity: digital entertainment.

Your detox provides space for your kids to throttle down to normal, real-life levels of brain stimulation. You've demolished the digital entertainment status quo. Now you are rebuilding their minds and hearts more intentionally. Reading aloud is the simplest and most effective way to help develop your kids' ability to sustain attention.

General language apprehension. Experts suggest that the single biggest indicator of a child's future success is the number of words a child hears from her caregiver between infancy and age three. In fact, one physician and author purports that the gap in academic achievement is due to the deficit in words spoken to babies in their first three years of life.[7] Young kids who hear the most language have the best chance at positive development. Before children have the ability to read, their parents are the primary source of spoken words. I don't know about you, but sometimes I run out of profound (or even coherent) thoughts and ideas. What a blessing to have a stack of timeless treasured stories that can step in. You only need to lend your reading voice.

Help your children become more proficient in written language. In *The Read-Aloud Handbook*, Jim Trelease distinguishes between two main forms of English: home language and standard language. Home language is used more frequently and conversationally. It is more rambling and imprecise than written or standard language. But the tremendous gift of teaching our children standard English cannot be overemphasized, as it "is the primary tongue of the classroom and business world."[8] Standard English is written English. Reading aloud familiarizes our kids with the lexicon, cadence, inflection, and style they will need as they grow older.

"Can't my child glean all of these benefits from a tablet that reads to them?"

In short, no. Technology can absolutely help our kids learn (more on this in chapter 9), but there is no substitute for an attentive parent. Aside from the obvious fact that tablets lack arms and laps, studies have shown that kids retain information better when they are learning from a physical book rather than an electronic book, *and* from a real, live person.

One study introduced Mandarin to nine-month-old American babies. One group of babies was exposed to the language in person by warm, motherly voices. The second group of babies heard the same Mandarin—which was also spoken with motherly warmth—but this time through audio or video. After twelve sessions, the babies who heard the language spoken through live people could recognize Mandarin. But the babies who heard the language through a recording? Nada.[9]

By every metric, books, reading aloud, and reading for pleasure will benefit your children in transformative ways. Reading is free and simple and will change your kids' lives. This two-week window is the perfect time to instill or rekindle a love of books in your kids, because the sustained attention required is not being lured away by electronics. Capitalize on this window, and your children will thank you.

DETOX OBSERVATIONS

Keep your journal nearby to jot down observations throughout your detox. The good, the bad, and the ugly. You'll refer to this later, when you create your family's long-term plan.

General observations

Hidden talents identified

Character aspects/virtues/qualities that could use some cultivating

Newfound book genres your kids love

Aspects from the detox you'd like to keep permanent

PART TWO

NOW WHAT?
SUSTAINING YOUR RESULTS

A goal without a plan is just a wish.

ANTOINE DE SAINT-EXUPÉRY

7

Creating a Long-Term Plan
for Younger Kids

Look, Dad! A tractor! Just like in the game Farm Simulator.

MY FIVE-YEAR-OLD CHILD WALKING INTO
HOME DEPOT, PRE-DETOX

Twelve-year-old children in the U.S. report spending an average
of less than 6 hours per week outdoors, which is less than the
average daily screen time for young people.

TASSIA K. OSWALD, ET AL.

CONGRATULATIONS! You just took on a massive counter-
cultural movement under your own roof. You may have been ter-
rified. There may have been weeping and gnashing of teeth on
detox eve. The kids may have even shed a tear too. But you did it!
Bravo. Seriously.

Over the last two weeks, you observed the good, the bad, and the ugly. You saw strengths and weaknesses in your kids with new-found clarity. There were victories and failures. Some aspects of your detox you will want to carry on forever. Other parts you might be relieved to have behind you.

Now comes the fun part. You get to create your own individual-ized, bespoke long-term plan. Today you have a whole new world of parental insight that you didn't have two weeks ago. Use it. Dad and Mom, no one on the planet is better suited to make these decisions. And in the pages ahead you'll find additional coaching to get you through the process.

Good parents teach their kids about the joys and perils of life in a digital world. They create a long runway to train, equip, and launch great kids into the world. Our tiniest kids will one day be grown, and we are creating opportunities to help them navigate and enjoy the exhilaration of a tech-rife world. We are helping to inform and develop their capacity for digital wisdom.

In this chapter, we are creating a runway. We are developing a long-term tech plan for our youngest kids. For most families, that means babies through elementary school. Plans for younger kids will look a little different than long-term plans for older kids (el-ementary and junior high school), who have been given their own devices or more access to different forms of technology. (More on the plan for older kids in the next chapter.)

A note on helicopter parenting

You might be worried that establishing rules about digital enter-tainment will get you labeled a helicopter parent. But limiting access to things that kids aren't developmentally ready for yet isn't helicopter parenting—it's good parenting.

Creating rules, even if they make you "stricter" than other par-ents, is not helicopter parenting. In fact, the approach we are after is the opposite. We are imparting instruction and wisdom in our children from a young age. We are showing them how the world works and creating opportunities for them to try, fail, and try again. This type of parenting creates kids who are *more* capable of responsibility at a younger age. We must be the scaffolding for our littlest humans as they learn how the world works and how to navigate life. Part of that means creating barriers around access to dangerous or harmful things, before kids have developed the discernment to make those decisions for themselves.

Creating your long-term plan

Step 1: Assess what you loved about detox mode

Your long-term plan is completely customizable. YOU are the person most qualified to decide what it will look like. *You* love your kids more than anyone and have their long-term interests at heart. *You* have observed the negative impacts of too much tech. And who was there for two weeks, observing your precious little people's natural talents, interests, and personality flaws? You again! (Possibly with input from grandparents, teachers, or babysitters.) You have studied your kids without any screens at all. You've done the hard work to take back the keys and get into the driver's seat. Media marketing doesn't dictate your parenting decisions. Your kids' friends do not wield parental authority in your home. If a fourth-grade classmate gets six hours of daily screen time and has his own iPhone, so what? That has nothing to do with your house. None of these factors get to make your parenting decisions for you.

You are going to make your plan thoughtfully and individually. You are the only one whose primary interest is your child's long-term well-being. And you've spent two weeks observing your kids without any tech as entertainment. Take a moment to jot some observations in your detox journal.

1. What surprised you?
2. What encouraged you?

3. What did you learn about your kids' interests and talents? (Examples: favorite book genres; hidden talents related to painting, storytelling, acting, cooking, drawing, soccer, juggling, gymnastics, karate, glassblowing, welding, birdhouse making, engineering, egg dying, whatever.)

4. What areas did you observe in your kids that need work? (Examples: Six-year-old Billy needs to practice taking turns; Sarah, age four, gets frustrated easily when she loses; Ernie, a fourth-grader, struggles to make back-and-forth conversation with other kids. Emily, age fourteen, can't make simple conversation with the cashier.)

5. What didn't you love? Where did you miss technology as a tool?

Step 2: Clarify your family's approach to technology

With your personal observations, jot down some big-picture principles for how you *want* tech to be used in your home.

Here are some principles that were clarified for my family— thanks to our detox:

> We want to use technology as a tool for real life, not to supplant real life.
>
> We want to use technology to help us connect with one another, not isolate from one another.
>
> We want technology to work for us, not to feel enslaved to it.
>
> When technology is stressing us out, we take a break.

Remember your family's guiding principles from chapter 1. Now look at your observations from your detox at the end of chapter 6. Holding the two together, you are going to create a long-term plan that helps you work toward your goals as a family. No more mindless digital consumption.

No more entertaining our kids instead of parenting them. No more wasting the time away. Your long-term plan is going to remove the crutch of passive screen use to help build resilient kids. Instead of numbing out on a video game to ignore sad feelings, your child is going to quietly think, and process those feelings with Mom or Dad. Instead of isolating with a glowing iPad screen, your child is going to take a walk and ask the neighbor to ride bikes. Instead of giving up on that LEGO compound and turning on Netflix, your child is going to press through the frustration—to go where no LEGO man has gone before. Every one of these exercises builds aspects of our kids' characters that they will use long after they have moved out and are living on their own.

Step 3: Determine ideal tech frequency

While determining tech frequency is only one component of a successful long-term plan, it is also the most critical one. The number of minutes you allow your child to use his device is the most tangible way to convey your plan. It's also the simplest way to measure digital entertainment doses. The frequency plan encompasses all tech use. (The second way to create your long-term plan is by tech type: phones, social media, video games. If you've chosen to give your child a phone, you'll need to consider both approaches. More on tech-type plans in the next chapter.)

Here are a few sample plans based on tech frequency. Write out in your detox notebook which plan (and any modifications) best fits your family's needs.

Continue screenless living indefinitely, for an extended detox

If you enjoy detox mode and your kids seem to be doing well, I highly recommend continuing. Continued detox mode will help you make a more informed long-term plan when you do jump back into the tech world. An extended detox will help your kids to see the tech fast as a lifestyle rather than a crash diet. Many experts recommend four- to six-week detoxes for kids, although our family and several other families observed results after only two weeks.

After our initial two-week detox, we decided to continue for a month. After the month passed, my husband and I extended the detox again—for four more months. Because we hadn't expressly told our kids how long our detox would last, we had the freedom to do this. I *highly* recommend this route. If your kids are young enough and it is reasonable to leave the time limit open-ended, DO IT. This was entirely feasible with five kids aged ten and under.

Small kids do not need to regularly spend time on screens. Just because iPads are available doesn't mean you have to give your kid one. I say this as a mom who used to allow two hours (or more!) per day of screens for my own young kids who were born within three years of each other. At the time, I didn't fully understand the damaging effects of screen time. Even though I witnessed negative behaviors after tech use, I didn't take the next step to ask a few simple questions and do a little research. I also assumed (wrongly) that problems only arose if iPad time displaced all other activities. If I simply balanced the few hours of daily tech time with other activities, everything would level out, right? Tablet time, Netflix, and video games gave me an opportunity to finish chores, I reasoned.

Knowing what I know now, I wish I had pulled the plug much sooner. I had no clue what was happening in my kids' brains that made screen time undesirable. Experts tell us that the cells being repeatedly used during these age windows will be hardwired, while the parts of the brain that aren't used begin to atrophy. So if kids are spending time overstimulated and inactive, tapping a screen repetitively, those couch potato "skills" will be hardwired. If during these windows of tremendous opportunity our kids are practicing piano or playing catch, those skills will be hardwired.[1]

Most experts across the liberal and conservative spectrum agree that kids should not have mobile devices until they are *at least* twelve years old.[2] This includes phones, tablets, laptops, iPod touch—any devices that allow kids to access the internet and social controls.

After approaching tech naively for too long, I am a fierce advocate of extending the screenless years for as long as possible. We ultimately maintained a strict digital detox for five months. That said, sometimes *my* ideal isn't perfect for every family. And that's okay! Let's look at some other sample long-term plans.

One hour of media use, one day per week

For younger children without social media or personal phones, this plan allows you the benefits of being 99.98 percent screen free. (A vast improvement from the status quo of eight hours per day, or 33 percent of the week, spent on screens!) One hour per week allows you to drastically reduce screen use, while also enabling your children to experience the hobbies they claim are their favorite. (Although with more time now available to explore the real world, that will likely change.) For this plan, you declare that Sunday or Saturday (or whatever day is best for your family) is the day the kids each get an hour of video game play or supervised YouTube.

Be mindful that even with limited tech use, kids will encounter inappropriate content. My oldest daughter was playing a video game on the family desktop in the kitchen during her one hour of weekly screen time. Another game avatar approached her to ask for her physical address. This could have been a child making socially unaware conversation, but possibly not. Either way, no one should be sharing their address with a stranger over the internet. (Unless it's an adult ordering UberEats. Technology is full of paradoxes.) My daughter knew that this was not okay, because we'd already had this conversation with her, and she told us immediately. Limiting tech time doesn't guarantee that your kids will not encounter garbage. Keep tech use in a family space so your kids feel protected and accountable.

One hour per weekend day

Parents Kim and Ben detoxed their three boys—six, eight, and ten—for thirty days. They put in hard work up front and observed the incredible results of their kids without any screens. After assessing the benefits of screenless life while also considering that their boys are video-game fans, they decided to allow one hour of video games per weekend day.

When you keep video-game time relegated to weekends, you won't argue about it during weekdays.

As you create your long-term plan, you need to weigh your kids' ages and needs. In our experience, most elementary-aged kids have zero need for daily screen entertainment. As kids grow older and a part of their social lives seems to migrate into the online world, this may change. Parents will need to be reasonable but not passive, drawing clear boundaries while also allowing space for kids to make some of their own decisions. More on this in the next chapter.

Exceptions that don't count toward tech frequency

Rules are so helpful to navigating the tech world, but we also don't want to be inflexible and legalistic. The goal is to make tech work for us, not to stress us out. Tech can be useful and enjoyable—in its right place.

Digital entertainment, together. Technology is at its best when we use it to connect with and enjoy people we love. Family movie nights, family Mario Kart tournaments, a joint game of Kahoot trivia. Exceptions like these might happen a few times per week. Each exception should be a discrete event with a defined starting and stopping time. For example, "Okay, kids, we are going to play four rounds of Mario Kart together." Or "We are going to watch *Lord of the Rings* tonight." You are not creating opportunities for mindless consumption of never-ending entertainment marathons. You are using technology as a venue to connect and share an experience together. Also, by setting expectations up front, you will have less arguing or negotiating when the movie ends.

When it's not your house. When our children go to a friend's house, they abide by the house rules of the parent in charge. This assumes that you trust the parents to set safe boundaries. If you aren't sure, it is okay to request that the kids avoid screen use. Or better yet, invite the other child to your house.

If your kids are going to a grandparent's house, have an open conversation with grandparents about the journey you've been on, and how much better behaved your kids have been without all the tech. Tell them what you've read about technology hurting kids. Ask if they'd be willing to maintain the limits you've set in place. Again, mind your tone in these conversations. It might be best if the spouse who is biologically related to the grandparents has this conversation. Sometimes in-law conversations can get sticky.

Tech as a tool. Parents of tweens have shared that several times per week their kids want to use technology for a legitimately great reason: "Mom? What does the Eiffel Tower look like?" "How long would it take us to get to India by airplane?" "Can I make a Google Slides presentation about minerals?" Keep your family computer in the kitchen. Our kids (all twelve and under) know that they aren't to sit and surf without permission or supervision. But when they ask for one of the above, and they do it in plain view of a supervising adult, why not? We let our kids use technology occasionally, as a tool to complete brief, specific tasks.

Step 4: Create great spaces

As you create your long-term plan, you want to make spaces to benefit your kids' short- and long-term development. Not only are you removing screens, but you will be filling the spaces that screens leave behind with worthwhile endeavors. As you saw during your detox, this doesn't require Mom and Dad to be camp counselors 24/7. But you will want to do a little work on the front end to create both headspace and physical space for them to problem-solve, create, imagine, explore, and grow.

When we call our kids out of their passive comfort zones, we are bringing them closer to achieving their true potential. There is a gap between their current abilities and what is possible. As parents, we have the privilege of coaching them from what they cannot do toward what they will be able to do one day. Help pull your kids into this space and give them the tools they need. Encourage the heck out of them. Watch the magic happen. But it all starts with creating spaces.

As you read through the following paragraphs, keep your journal handy and jot down specific time and location ideas for your kids to invest time in the following spaces, based on how they are uniquely wired.

Outside spaces. Studies have shown that improving your attention span, sharpening your memory, and bolstering thinking skills is directly correlated with spending time in nature.[3] Helping our kids think more clearly and feel calmer is as simple as going outside. But parents didn't need a study to know this was true. We were able to observe it in our own kids, who went from occasional swamp creature (pre-detox) to charming explorer, roaming the lawn in search of ladybugs.

Sometimes we overcomplicate this. Get comfortable creating ideas on the fly. Hand your child a paper bag and tell her to collect red objects from the yard. Give her a seed from your apple and have her plant it. Suggest the kids build a fairy fort under that overgrown bush out back. Mark six different colors on a paper bag, and have your kids find one of each color object (a gray pebble, a brown leaf, a red piece of lint). Have them collect different leaves and rub them with crayons. Options are endless!

For more ideas about outdoor activities for your kids, refer to the list you made during your detox, or download a free list of ideas from my website, www.mollydefrank.com.

Reading spaces. Research repeatedly shows us that frequency and depth of reading are enormous predictors of future success. Create settings that champion reading. In doing so, you are not only promoting literacy, but building your kids' capacity for empathy, understanding cause and effect, self-control, virtue, and more.

Gather a pile of pillows and set them in front of the sunny spot by the window. Call it a reading nook. Lay a blanket on the lawn. Sit with your toddler and read a few books aloud. Then leave the books and let them flip through, pointing out specific colors, pictures of people, vehicles, animals.

Spaces for honing responsibility. Too many teenagers today are less productive and more entertained than ever before. Let's set our youngest kids on a different trajectory. Maybe your children are too small for legal employment, but it's never too early to help them understand the joy and responsibility of doing a job well and managing their money. Maybe they can come up with their own business plan, offering additional household chores to earn some cash. (Not to be confused with the basic household responsibilities that we do not need to pay our kids for.)

Encourage your kids to brainstorm ideas to improve the household: organizing the bookshelf, sweeping the porch, fluffing the pillows, putting away the laundry. We all have a natural bent toward easy. Who wants to put effort in when we could lie on the couch? We must train our kids to take pride in their spaces and to look for ways to bless their family and home. Instill a love of serving in your kids. The best way to do this is to encourage, notice, and praise.

Socializing spaces. In real life. With real people. In real conversations. Face-to-face, sans devices. Real conversations that include lulls and plenty of awkwardness. Sherry Turkle is an MIT professor who has been researching the impact of tech on society for thirty years. One of her bestselling books chronicled both the damaging effect of tech on humanity as well as the cure. What does she say is the cure for a tech-saturated world? Brain surgery? A magic elixir? Dumping every device into the ocean? Nope. *Conversation.*[4] Phew! We can totally do that!

Create spaces for your kids to have friends over, meet at the park, bike to the dirt lot, and ruminate together with a friend. Don't overcomplicate it. They do not need a headset or Call of Duty to facilitate social interactions. Plan a hangout for your daughter and her friend. Teach them the art of the lanyard keychain. Invite your son's friend over to play soccer, build LEGO, or skateboard.

Bottom line

When it comes to digital entertainment for our young kids, less is best. With lots of parental love, attention, and firm boundaries, we can help our young kids navigate technology well. If you're wondering what that looks like in the tween and early teen years, keep reading. In the next chapter I will share a promising example of a tech-savvy, happy, and relational eighteen-year-old woman whose parents' long-term plan proved successful. The path is there—we simply need to find it and walk it.

THINK TWICE BEFORE GIVING YOUR CHILD A SMARTPHONE

When we had our first child in 2009, the iPhone had only been around two years. The iPad was a symbol of affluence, and the concept of children having a phone in their pocket seemed so tech-forward and expensive—but the best chance your kid would have for a bright future in a digital world.

A lot has changed since then. We've observed an entire generation of kids grow up with their own smartphones. In a sense, the kids are "brighter," with faces continually lit up by a glowing screen. The results have been disappointing, as the research has shown.

We've taken a generation of kids during their most socially vulnerable years—they've been looking for validation—and we've handed them an impossible place to find it: access to the entire world, to every middle-aged creep posing as a teenager. We've handed a generation of kids a phone—full access to pornography, bullying, and endless opportunities to be peer-pressured into sending naked pictures. Regret can't undo the damage.

Why are we putting our kids in these situations? Today's parents won't let their fourteen-year-olds walk through the mall with a group of friends without a parent, but they have no qualms sending their child to bed with a smartphone. Seventy-two percent of preteens and eighty-two percent of teens sleep with their phones beside them.[5] Our kids are living in a waking nightmare under our own roofs—being bullied, sending and receiving explicit photos, getting direct messages from sex offenders posing as teenagers.

Parents want what's best for their kids. For a long time, we thought that giving our kids the newest technology *was* best for them. The marketing machine has worked tirelessly to get us to spend our money, and they've weaponized our kids against us. In pursuit of education and connection, we have dumped more money than we'd wished. What do we have to show for it? Our kids are more depressed, more suicidal, less social, and unprepared for the real world. Something tells me we've been duped.

But hope is not lost. As more information becomes available, we reassess. It's okay to change your mind if you've taken a wrong turn. In fact, it's the mark of logic and reason.

After observing that more tech isn't best for our kids, we know better. The studies have shown us this on a macro scale. Through your detox, you've observed it on a micro scale. Now that we know better, we can do better. After a decade of handing kids smartphones, I believe the tide will turn, because we've seen that the marketing machine has not delivered the results we were promised.

For now, my husband and I have decided there will be no smartphones for our kids, who are age twelve and under. In the interest of full disclosure, our kids do not like this. If we allowed them to create the rules in our home, the rules would be different. But my husband and I lose exactly no sleep over this decision, because we know that it is for their good.

As kids grow older and we see new ways for technology to help us function better as a family, there are better options than smartphones. A non-smartphone is one great option. Many look like smartphones. They allow music, phone, messaging, contacts, optional camera, video, gallery, calendar, calculator, clock, voice recorder, FM radio. But there is no app store or internet browsing option. This setup allows kids to use technology as a tool, rather than getting sucked into an entertainment and temptation vortex.

At some point, we want to train our kids to use the available technology well, while they are still under our roof. We will decide—on a child-by-child basis—when each kid is ready for a smartphone. And even then, it will be incrementally allowed. It is never wise to give any child immediate, full, and unfettered access to the entire world.

A nonprofit group called Wait Until 8th urges parents to take a pledge to wait until their kids are in *at least* eighth grade before giving them smartphones. The organization suggests that parents wait until their kids are sixteen before getting them a data plan. Their mission is backed by countless experts. Wait Until 8th's website allows parents to sign their pledge. Once ten parents from the same school and grade have signed the pledge, it becomes "active." From the website:

> The pledge will empower parents to rally together to delay the smart-phone at least until 8th grade. By banding together, this will decrease the pressure within the child's grade to have a smartphone. By signing the online pledge, you promise not to give your child a smartphone until at least 8th grade as long as at least 10 families total from your child's grade and school pledge. Once 10 families have pledged to delay the smartphone, you will be notified that the pledge is in effect![6]

What a great way to garner accountability and support from and for other parents who care about protecting their kids in a world drowning in tech.

You might find yourself on the forefront of this trend in your child's school. For many post-detox parents, the hardest aspect of their long-term plan is that their child is the "only one" who isn't allowed to have a smartphone. If parents come together, they create support rather than pressure to cave to the status quo. I highly recommend recruiting friends to come along this journey with you.

Your kids will encounter porn online

A few years ago on Instagram, someone asked tech expert and motivational speaker Collin Kartchner what age kids should get a smartphone. Collin replied that it should be whatever age parents are ready for them to start looking at porn.[7]

Culture Reframed, a nonprofit organization that works to equip parents to navigate the "public health crisis of the digital age," shares the following:

- One-third of kids today have seen porn by age twelve.
- Porn-based websites get more monthly visitors than Amazon, Twitter, and Netflix *combined*.
- One-third of internet downloads are pornography related.
- Studies show that kids who access pornography are more depressed, struggle to bond with parents, have low self-esteem and struggle with body image, and are more likely to experience social, emotional, and sexual problems as adults.[8]

Today's parents cannot afford to ignore the reality of growing up in a digital world. It is only a matter of time before our kids are exposed to explicit images online. Jesus said that to look with lust at a person who is not your spouse is to commit adultery in your heart (Matthew 5:28). The very next thing he said? If your right eye or right hand is making you stumble, throw it out. If a kid's smartphone is causing them to make poor choices, the next step is obvious.

Accessing porn is easier than it's ever been, and there's less accountability than ever before. No wonder it's so prevalent. These images are designed to titillate, and human beings are wired to enjoy sex. It's not complicated. A person is not weird or crazy if they desire to look at something designed to excite them. From a Christian perspective, to allow or seek pleasure in something that God has expressly forbidden is sin. Teaching our children to seek God and run from sin is our job as parents. We must protect and educate our kids in this arena. Why shouldn't they look? Why are these images wrong? Why do they exist in the first place? If we don't educate our kids, they will ask Google or their friends.

Secular studies show that viewing porn has detrimental health effects. No parent wants their kids to feel unequipped when they encounter explicit images. Instead, we want our kids to think, "Oh, this is that thing my parents told me would be on here. I know what I'm supposed to do when I see it." We must prepare them. As much as developmentally appropriate, we must provide context for God's design for sex before our kids encounter the kinds of images they will readily find in the dumpster fire that is the internet. If you're not ready to talk with your kids about these topics, they are not ready to be left alone with any smartphone, tablet, or computer. Kids who avoid or condemn pornography will be going against the grain. If we want our children to say no to the destructive images and videos that will inevitably show up, we must educate and empower them to do so.

See the Recommended Reading list in the back of the book for contextualizing and informing your children.

8

Creating a Long-Term Plan
for Older Kids

I worry that the level of interruption, the sort of overwhelming
rapidity of information . . . is in fact altering cognition.

ERIC SCHMIDT, FORMER CEO, GOOGLE

Thirteen-year-old Athena . . . after her summer of Netflix, texting,
and social media holed up in her room [says,] "My bed has, like,
an imprint of my body."

JEAN M. TWENGE, *IGEN*

"YOU HAVE CAVITIES in every single tooth," the dentist told
the teenager in the chair adjacent to us. The girl was probably
fourteen. "And these are your permanent teeth. You should be
brushing three times a day. You should stop all sugary drinks and
snacks. Water only, okay?" The dentist sounded exasperated. My
three-year-old foster son quietly inspected his new toothbrush as
he waited for his checkup. I glanced up at the teenager on the

receiving end of the lecture. She was staring at her phone, completely unresponsive to the dentist. Her shirt said, "I came. I saw. I got anxiety. I left." She continued to ignore the dentist, who repeated her speech at least twice (probably because her audience was ignoring her). "Also, the root canal we did on that back tooth? That tooth is almost rotted. I don't know what else to say. . . ."

My kids have had cavities despite regular brushing, so I didn't want to be too judgmental. But this situation sounded like a disaster. *Why isn't this girl even responding to the dentist? Why does Mom allow her child to eat garbage and ruin her teeth? What is going on?*

Finally, it was our turn for an exam. The dentist informed me that my foster son had a few small cavities between his teeth. "I can tell he's brushing, but he needs to floss more. You'll want to schedule those fillings so they don't get worse."

"Okay, thanks. We definitely have room for improvement on the flossing front." I looked around and saw that the place was empty. "Any chance you could do the fillings now?" I asked. "It would be nice to get that taken care of, so they don't get worse."

"I do have time in my schedule. I can do them today, as long as he is okay with it." She motioned to my three-year-old foster son. "Does *he* mind if we fill them now?"

Huh? I thought. She wants me to ask a three-year-old permission to take a drill to his teeth? I looked back at her for a moment to make sure she wasn't kidding. She held my gaze, waiting for me to get approval. I turned to my preschooler, still in disbelief. The dentist watched. "Hey, buddy . . . you did such a great job with your cleaning. Now we are going to get those cavities filled for you . . . okay?"

"Okay!" he said, bouncing his goody bag around.

Thankfully, my quasi-request and preschooler's subsequent "consent" were enough for the dentist. "Okay, let's fill those cavities!"

I began to understand the problem.

Kids' preferences and appetites are driving parenting decisions like never before. Parents aren't parenting. We are allowing children to make decisions they lack the experience and wisdom to make. This is not helping our kids. In fact, it's harming them.

Dr. Leonard Sax is a practicing family physician, psychologist, and bestselling author. In his book *The Collapse of Parenting*, he proposes that today's teens are less resilient, more disrespectful, and less equipped for life in the real world. The reason? Parents have abdicated their role as primary influencers of their kids.[1] Instead, teens are looking to each other for understanding their place in the world and cultural norms. Teen social media celebrities are literally called "influencers." And teens are spending upwards of nine hours *per day* being influenced by internet strangers.

Canadian psychologist Dr. Gordon Neufeld observes, "For the first time in history, young people are turning for instruction, modeling, and guidance not to mothers, fathers, teachers, and other responsible adults but to people whom nature never intended to place in a parenting role—their own peers. . . . Children are being brought up by immature persons who cannot possibly guide them to maturity. They are being brought up by each other."[2]

Fifteen-year-old kids raising each other? What could go wrong? (If you're picturing *Lord of the Flies*, digital version, you are not alone.)

Hope for parenting tweens in a digital world

Peyton is an eighteen-year-old senior in high school. Her parents gave her a phone when she began playing travel volleyball in junior high so they could coordinate pickups and drop-offs. The phone was only programmed for texts and phone calls. All other apps were off-limits, until Peyton demonstrated over time that she could handle more responsibility.

For years, Peyton's parents checked her phone whenever they wanted, a condition of her having a phone in the first place. As she now prepares to head to college, her parents no longer do random phone checks. According to her parents, friends, and teachers, Peyton is responsible and kind, a woman of strong character. She is a leader in youth group, is popular, and gets solid grades.

Parents of younger kids look at older kids like Peyton and think, *How do we get there from here?* We all want to launch responsible kids into the world when they're eighteen—kids who have had enough experience with technology while at home so that Mom and Dad can coach, mentor, and counsel. But not kids who are sucked into the entertainment vortex.

I asked Peyton—who has witnessed many peers make regrettable decisions with their iPhones—to tell me what her parents did well. Why didn't she make the kinds of mistakes that her peers did? Online bullying, sexting, hiding fake social media accounts from parents, becoming enslaved to a device. With a phone in her pocket, she had every opportunity to make similar decisions. Why didn't she?

Peyton credits her parents for her ability to navigate the cutthroat digital waters. "My parents talk to me about *everything*. Aside from telling me and my sister about the kinds of images and messages we'd see online, they provided context for it," she said.

Peyton also wisely noted that when parents give a child a smartphone, they're handing over access to the entire world. Bad decisions made online don't originate online; they come from a deeper heart issue. Because of that, Peyton believes it's easier for kids to make better decisions when they are "given more freedom little by little, rather than all at once."

Along the way, parents must warn their kids to look out for the triggers and stressors that can lead their hearts and thoughts down a bad trail.

"My mom always encourages me to guard my heart," said Kendall, Peyton's fifteen-year-old sister. "We will see certain things online that are unavoidable. And it's going to bring up a lot of ugly comparison issues. My mom told me to be mindful of that, so I don't get sucked into it," she said.

Both girls agreed that their parents' successful approach to tech was rooted in something deeper than a simple phone policy.

Moms and Dads: We must frame the conversation and provide a moral compass for our kids. And we must do this *before* they're given access to life online. Otherwise, you've willingly handed your powerful torch of influence to any random YouTuber or social media celebrity.

The recipe for success is clear: Set firm boundaries and require obedience of your tiniest kids from day one, *while* investing in them relationally. Parents are the naturally appointed primary source of influence and insight for their kids. We simply have to do the job we've already been given. As our kids grow older, the rules eventually fade, but our relationship with them is forever.

Your long-term plan will be created under the umbrella of both firm boundaries and healthy relationship.

Step 1: Recount what you loved about detox mode

After tracking your parental observations about the detox, talk to your kids! Ask what they loved and didn't love about their detox. If your kids understand that you are legitimately interested in their input, and that you're not gathering ammo to use against them, they will be honest with you. Ask how they felt emotionally and mentally when they weren't numbed out on excessive tech entertainment. Were they less stressed? Older kids might have suffered from FOMO (fear of missing out), which is entirely relatable.

Were they more productive without a constant diversion in their pockets? What specifically did they miss when their devices weren't an option? If they answer, "My phone," dig deeper. Was it connecting with friends? Was it updates on baseball scores? Was it their posting streak on TikTok? Get underneath that expressed desire and into the heart issue. Do they want to feel seen? Understood?

Popular? Do they want to express themselves? To feel validated? Important? These are such understandable desires for our kids. You are seeking to identify which desires drive *your* kid to screens so you can find better ways to meet those desires without a screen.

Brainstorm with your kids some ideas for meeting their needs in ways that don't involve screens. The tone of this conversation is critical. Your kids should feel completely listened to, and their feedback needs to be lovingly, thoroughly considered. But they should know that the ultimate decision will be up to Mom and Dad.

Open up your journal and jot down observations and ideas from you and your kids as you begin to formulate your long-term plan.

For Mom and Dad

1. What did you love about the detox?
2. What parts of technology did you miss?

Spend some time talking through these with your spouse.

Dad Robert recounted the following after his eleven-year-old son's detox:

> Several times in the past couple months, prior to the screen break, I had to drag him out of the house and force him to go on a short run around the block with me because he would otherwise lounge around the house in between the screen time we allowed him. He would complain during the entire run. This week, on his own initiative, he established a workout schedule that he's abiding by on his own. Yesterday, he asked me to go running with him! He led the run and took us about two or three times farther than I normally had to force him to run pre–screen break. He's generally had a better attitude, without the Xbox hangover we're all used to. And this morning I think I actually heard him talking about a book he's reading.

I interviewed this eleven-year-old, who happens to be a great kid. He admitted that his mood was better during detox mode. Mom and Dad used their observations to create a long-term plan that removed video gaming from weekdays. "Since we did that, he's lost some interest in Xbox for sure. He doesn't even use all his allotted time anymore," his mom told me. Instead, he's taking part in more worthwhile activities.

For the children

1. What are three things you enjoyed about detox mode?
2. Name something you did during the detox that you wouldn't have done, made, or accomplished if you'd had the option to play video games or scroll on your phone.
3. What was the hardest part of detox mode?

Note: Before you utter a word about screen plans, prepare delicious food. This is a parenting hack that's been studied and proven. People like things and people that they encounter while eating. It's called the luncheon technique.[3] Once you have your pizza, smoothies, or popcorn, you are ready for your conversation.

Validate the validatable

As you listen and discuss your children's observations, validate the good points they make. If a child says she felt less anxious or depressed during her detox, you can tell her she isn't alone.

Jean Twenge, a San Diego State University psychology professor, has done the research to prove it:

> Teens who spend more time on screen activities . . . are more likely to be unhappy, and those who spend more time than average on nonscreen activities . . . are more likely to be happy. There's not a single exception: all screen activities are linked to less happiness,

and all nonscreen activities are linked to more happiness. For example, 8th graders who spend ten or more hours a week on social media are 56% more likely to be unhappy than those who don't. Admittedly, ten hours a week is a lot—so what about those who spend merely six hours a week or more on social media? They are still 47% more likely to say they are unhappy. But the opposite is true of in-person social interaction: those who spend more time with their friends in person are 20% *less* likely to be unhappy.[4]

Share the data with your kids. Tweens are learning how to process truth and data, how to implement facts of reality in their own lives. Help them. If your child admits her mind was clearer or she felt less sad during her detox—listen. Do not respond with "I told you so." Respond in the way that you would to a friend who shared the same. "That's really interesting you say that. I recently read that science backs up your feelings! Can I read you this paragraph? Really mind-blowing. Can you think of how you've seen this play out with friends?"

Thirteen-year-old Athena told Dr. Twenge, "I've seen my friends with their families—they don't talk to them. . . . They just say, 'Okay, okay, whatever,' while they're on their phones. They don't pay attention to their family."[5] If your child shares an observation like this about her own friends, ask what she thought about the scene. Is that the kind of interactions she wants to have in your home? Or does she want something different? What types of family interactions are the most life-giving for her? Give your teens some opportunities to brainstorm ways to create the environment that promotes the kinds of interactions they want.

Real-life example

Parents of fourteen-year-old Ava implemented a digital detox, despite Ava's objections. After two weeks, I asked Ava to share some observations with me. What did she love?

"I was so productive! I read four 600-page books. I cleaned out my desk. I memorized a new song on my guitar. Overall, I felt less stressed. I didn't even miss having my phone. It's so easy to pick up my phone and scroll, but during my detox that wasn't an option, so instead I went on four-mile walks."

Ava enjoyed her screen-free two weeks. Believe it or not, most teens and tweens who try the detox admit that it was a positive experience. Like other kids have reported, she was happier, more confident, and generally in a better mood during her detox. I asked Ava if there were any aspects of her detox she wanted to keep for the long term.

"Well, I don't want to watch TV during the day," she said. "My mom already decided this for me, but even if she hadn't, I would have wanted to get rid of it and only watch a show or two at night with my family."

Spend some time drawing out your kids' observations in their own words. As these growing kids learn about the practical cause and effect of their choices, their motivation shifts from extrinsic to intrinsic. Instead of avoiding overuse of screen time because "Dad will be mad," their detox gives them a taste of clear headspace and productivity. Your kids will begin to desire what's better as they experience the joy of real-life connection, accompanying a sibling on a chore when they didn't have to, preparing a snack for the family. They are growing in digital wisdom!

Step 2: Create intentional spaces for kids to connect with you and with each other

Your long-term plan is going to rearrange the setup so your kids won't turn to screen diversions when they are bored, hurting, sad, lonely, or anxious. We want to create an atmosphere and habits where our kids continually and daily practice healthy habits of troubleshooting and talking through their normal human trials and emotions. Too often we make the mistake of entertaining our kids when we should be parenting them. An effective long-term plan is going to help you break this habit.

Instead of leaving your daughter to bury her feelings in a self-defeating TikTok binge, invite her to sit at the kitchen table and talk it through. Why should she watch hundreds of strangers' happy, beautiful highlight reels when she could sit next to Mom and process her feelings in the comforting presence of a parent who cares? The second scenario is obviously preferable. But our kids may not see that right now. Sometimes they need a parental nudge, even if they don't agree. *Especially* when they don't agree.

Build in specific times and spaces for regular connection with Mom and Dad (without phones). Some ideas to get you started:

Family dinner. Whether it's Top Ramen or a recipe from Julia Child, meals spent connecting with your kids have shown to drastically improve kids' relationships with their parents. The more often, the better. (Remember the luncheon technique!)

Morning sunrise hot cocoa and sunrise chat or Bible reading. This can be daily, weekly, or somewhere in the middle.

Jog, bike ride, or walk. This can fit into any schedule and physical ability level.

Cook together. Tell your twelve-year-old that you need her to bring her guacamole-making skills to the kitchen every Taco Tuesday. Help her develop a signature dish, and watch her beam while the family enjoys the fruits of her labor. Use the lulls between mashing to ask about her life.

Uno night. This can be weekly on a set date, or you can simply declare that this Saturday night is Uno night.

Drive. Through the hillside, to the grocery store, through the Starbuck's drive-through and back home again. It doesn't matter where you go when you're creating good old-fashioned windshield time.

Prune a tree, stack firewood, pull weeds. This one might not elicit as much excitement on the front end, but you will both be pleasantly surprised by the feeling of accomplishing a physical task together.

Book club. Find a book that you and your child might love. Then read it together. This can be aloud or separately, following a reading plan. Sit down together once a week and share your observations about the story, characters, what made you laugh or cry.

There may be a little pushback when you suggest any new activity. That's okay. Keep pressing through. Remember, you are the parent. Keep going. Soon her "favorite app" might be the kind she orders at dinner with family. (Chips and guac, anyone?)

Step 3: Parse out your approaches to different types of technology

If your kids are a little older, or already have their own personal phone, social media accounts, etc., you will need to create your long-term plan based on type of technology *and* frequency of use. (For more on tech frequency-based plans, flip back to the previous chapter.) Bring your older kids in on these discussions.

Conversations about limiting things your kids enjoy can be tense. Let's see if we can mitigate some of that tension. I created a tool in the back of the book to help keep everyone on task and hopefully avoid unnecessary conflict (see page 231, "Worksheet for Tweens and Teens"). In the same way good parents help their kids learn to track, spend, and save money, you are teaching your tweens and teens how to track, spend, and save time when it comes to digital entertainment consumption.

On the worksheet, your child might say she enjoys listening to music, learning to play new music, creating videos, watching Netflix, spending time on social media, texting with friends, playing video games. These can all be good uses of technology. Affirm that. And use your child's thoughts and feedback to create and explain your long-term plans for each type of technology, when appropriate.

Smartphones

Remember, we are not arguing that technology is bad. We love technology—in its right place. What are the right places for our kids' smartphones? These devices can be a powerful source of distraction and zombie-mode enablers. They can also be helpful tools. Helping our growing kids navigate the allure of tech is a massive calling in our modern world. But you have everything you need to make the best decision for your kids.

Clarify this for them. Explain the purpose of giving them a phone in the first place. Maybe that includes connecting with friends, staying in contact with Mom and Dad, taking photos, tracking school assignments. Yes, fun diversions will be included in this list. (Who doesn't love a good face-swap filter? Also, try slow-mo recording a willing participant vigorously shaking his face . . . and then play back for all to enjoy.) But neither of you would honestly say that the purpose of a phone is for someone to be entertained alone for the majority of his waking hours. If a phone is not serving the purpose it was intended to serve, you will need to reevaluate its use. That's what you're doing now.

You will earn major credibility points with your kids if you can humbly admit your own vulnerabilities. Not a person among us is immune to the allure of this tiny rectangular dopamine factory that fits in our pockets. Share some of your struggles and how you have overcome those—the boundaries you've put in place to help yourself.

One day, you won't be there to erect rules or standards. But today is not that day. Right now, your job is to lead them through the tech jungle, pointing out hazards, observing where unhealthy paths lead, and directing them on the right path.

Consider the "dumb phone"

When it comes to phones, wait longer and start simpler. If your child needs a way to call or text you in case of emergencies,

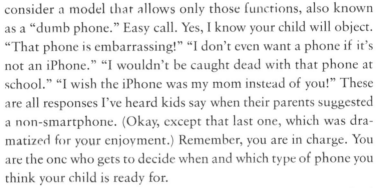

The digital entertainment we consume

- should facilitate real-life connection with actual people
- should support wonder and learning
- should enhance real life, not replace it
- should not use up all our free time
- should not make us feel depressed or anxious
- should not make us feel tethered to a device
- should not entail hours of isolated consumption

consider a model that allows only those functions, also known as a "dumb phone." Easy call. Yes, I know your child will object. "That phone is embarrassing!" "I don't even want a phone if it's not an iPhone." "I wouldn't be caught dead with that phone at school." "I wish the iPhone was my mom instead of you!" These are all responses I've heard kids say when their parents suggested a non-smartphone. (Okay, except that last one, which was dramatized for your enjoyment.) Remember, you are in charge. You are the one who gets to decide when and which type of phone you think your child is ready for.

Parents Bill and Gina gifted their thirteen-year-old son Michael a non-smartphone for his birthday. Michael is an incredible kid, kind, respectful, and friendly. He had been requesting a smartphone for months. His parents thoughtfully decided that despite cultural trends, handing a thirteen-year-old access to the entire universe was not, in fact, smart. At the moment of truth, Michael peeled back the birthday wrapping paper, revealing his brand-new dumb phone. To say he was deflated would be an understatement. He went to bed early, declining his own birthday cake. Gina felt terrible. But when Michael woke up the next morning, he took a closer look at his new phone. He realized that he could text his friends, make calls, take photos, and listen to music. The phone looked like any other smartphone. Soon enough, he expressed gratitude for this generous gift. Months later, Gina shares that she was deeply relieved that she and Bill didn't cave and get Michael the iPhone. "Now I don't feel stressed out all the time that he's getting into trouble, wondering what he's downloading or which videos he's streaming. I wish that more parents would do this. It would create less pressure for other parents." Certainly, our kids will encounter enough trouble on their own. No need for us to hand them a tool to make it easier.

Other personal devices with internet connection

Tablets, iPods, laptops, and computers with internet connections all have the same capacity to impact our kids in the way smartphones do. Often, I hear parents say that their kids are too young for a smartphone—yet they will allow the same child unsupervised access to a larger screen with the exact capabilities of a phone. The only difference is that it doesn't fit in the child's pocket. The child is now exposed to every danger that a smartphone enables—except that it can't dial up Grandma the old-fashioned way. How is this a better option for our younger kids? "Sweetie, this pocketknife is too dangerous for an eight-year-old to take to bed. . . . Here, take this machete with you instead. Good night!"

We need to treat all devices that connect to the internet the same way we treat smartphones: like a Pandora's box that opens access to the entire world. We must put loving limits and boundaries in place while our kids are still growing in wisdom. Our kids need us to roll up our sleeves and do our jobs.

Social media

What age should you allow a child to create an Instagram, TikTok, or other social media account?

Most social media platforms have user terms that prohibit children under thirteen from having an account. So not before then. Otherwise, we would be teaching our tween child that rules don't apply to them. If your child is younger than thirteen, the topic shouldn't even be up for consideration.

Even after a child turns thirteen, a numerical milestone doesn't mean that he or she has the tools and wisdom for social media. Parents will need to gauge their kids individually to determine if they have the wisdom and emotional stability to handle the content they will encounter—sexualized images of young girls, suggestive jokes, nudity, graphic images, bullying. How will your child respond to this? This type of content will bring up body image concerns, anxiety, stress, comparison, lack of gratitude, pressure to conform. These feelings are not new to the tech era, but their abundance and accessibility are. We don't want to expose our children to any of this before they have enough wisdom to categorize and value what they are seeing. Data shows that social media is more likely to cause depression in the youngest teens. Older teens who have developed more confidence tend to be less emotionally impacted by social media.[6] Waiting longer helps prevent the risk of depression and anxiety in your vulnerable tweens. We want our kids to have already cultivated the skill of taking in something new, considering it, and then deciding whether to hold on to it or throw it out as garbage—before we allow them to access a treasure box of garbage and gems mixed together.

Back in the digital stone age of the 1990s, television ratings and censors prevented kids from exposure to X-rated content. These protections are no longer guarding our kids' media consumption. This reality requires us to become a little savvier and nimbler than our parents were. We are up for the task. It starts with knowing your kids and erecting barriers that make it easier for them to adhere to the standards you've called them to. Before you allow an app, download it for yourself and scope it out. I tried this with TikTok. As I began scrolling, I was struck by two things: (1) Many people on the internet are hilarious and awesome. (I follow several cooks, comedians, and a housekeeper on this platform. The housekeeper has revolutionized my mopping technique.) (2) Parents are the new rating system. Explicit language, sexual content, glorification of drug use—it is everywhere. Dads and Moms must do the legwork; we must do the research.

Your job is to know your children's vulnerabilities, coaching them through the online world once they're ready for it. You are their training wheels. But remember that the stakes of online life are much higher than scraped knees. Err on the side of caution.

Video games

Two doctors and a lawyer were playing video games in the garage. No, that's not the beginning of a joke; it's what happens twice a month at my house. My husband and two of his high school buddies hang out and play video games for a few hours. They talk about life, work, and their kids. They play a game they all enjoy while connecting with each other. What a great use of technology.

As I mentioned a few chapters ago, we enjoy Mario Kart tournaments as a family. There is nothing inherently wrong with every video game. But we must be mindful when we permit our children to use anything with the addictive pull characteristic of newer video games.

We are trying to create the kinds of barriers and spaces that will prevent the development of professional couch potatoes. We are aiming to cultivate the best in our kids. Do the habits of your home cultivate entertainment consumption, or do they cultivate your kids' real-life giftings? Certainly, you can find a way to allow video games without surrendering your child's potential.

This will entail limiting game play while simultaneously feeding other gifts. For example, you might host a few of your child's friends for a monthly video-game night. But there's no need for the games to be played the entire time. With a few steps, you can easily pull this off for tweens. "Welcome, kids! Pizza arrives in an hour. Until then the basketball hoop is open, or you guys could play soccer out back. Video games will begin at seven-thirty." It could simply be a house rule that no video games are allowed on weekdays, and only for two specified hours on weekends, or whatever limit you set. With clear boundaries, your kids will have less difficulty explaining this to friends. "My parents are kind of strict with video games. We can only play Saturdays between seven and eight. The console won't even connect to the internet outside those hours. I know . . ." Maybe they'll shake their heads. Maybe they'll commiserate that parents just don't understand. Then they'll probably say something like, "Well . . . want to go throw the football?"

Shortly after our detox, my daughter had a friend over to play one afternoon. The friend asked me if the girls could play Minecraft. She could play on the kitchen computer, she suggested, while my daughter played on the living room TV. This sounded like a waste of a playdate to me. So I simply told her, "We're actually not doing video games today. But I'd love to help you guys think of something fun to do! You could bake this box of muffin mix, play hide and seek, color, listen to music." The child was visibly disappointed. But after a minute of brainstorming, she moved on to a different activity. My daughter and her friend had a great time on the trampoline, bouncing and laughing their heads off.

Each child will be a little different in terms of how much video-game stimulation they can handle without negative results. One dad reports that his elementary-aged child has dropped to the floor in a tantrum puddle after any amount of video-game play. He shared that his older child can play for an hour once a week without incident. Another parent shared that during an hour-long video-game session, her first grader had a bathroom accident because he didn't want to put down the remote control. The child had never struggled with potty issues, except while video gaming.

Gauge your kids. Remember the opportunity costs, and what you are aiming to cultivate.

There are infinite ways for our kids to relax without excessive video-game usage.

You are aiming to find that balance for your household, bearing your long-term goals in mind. Your children's aim will be to maximize momentary enjoyment. They are still learning about delaying gratification and why it's important to hone other skills. You *will* meet resistance when you limit their video games by any measure at all. Make peace with that. You know your children best, and you care more than anyone about their long-term development. Create your rules and boundaries with loving confidence. It's your job. You've got this.

Bottom line

The key to guiding our kids through the tech jungle is to maintain firm, loving, and age-appropriate rules *while* cultivating a great relationship with them. Relationship doesn't mean permissiveness; it means continual open and honest conversation.

Jen, mom to Peyton from earlier in this chapter, urges parents, "Have a good relationship with your kids. When both parents invest in strong relationships with their kids, the kids will not want to let their parents down. That is worth its weight in gold. And it helps kids when they are tempted."

We must create our long-term plans on the bedrock of relationship. If our guidelines and rules do not stem out of deep, abiding relationships in which our kids feel known and cherished, we will crash and burn.

When your kids see how loved they are, how interested you are in their lives, how delighted you are to be their parents, they will trust that you have their best interests at heart. As we invest in the lives of our favorite people, each instance of eye contact, listening earnestly to their hearts' burdens, sharing stories—every interaction—matters. They are building blocks of our relationships with tweens and teens who feel loved, cherished, and cared for. These are the teens who tell their parents everything, who are willing to honestly share their lives, and who will be more likely to adhere to parental rules, because they trust that they aren't arbitrary, but loving.

Maybe your kids are currently in a place where simply asking them if they are enslaved to their phones will elicit an honest response. If not, and if you need to put some more structure in place as they figure out what is best, let's create a framework.

If your kids aren't on the same page yet

When I was a kid, I would routinely ask my mom for a snack in the hour before dinner. Mom would always say the same thing: "You can have a piece of fruit." Even the memory of this interaction makes me want to throw my body to the ground in a childish, floppy-armed tantrum. "Fruit?! Come on, man!" I would protest. But you know what? Mom knew what she was talking about. She set a rule in place for my good. Thirty years later, when I am famished in the hour before a meal, I eat a piece of fruit. I wanted Cheetos; she gave me an apple. She cared enough to look past my complaining, to invest in the long term, to instill good habits that would continue for life.

Sometimes, when our willpower isn't strong enough to say no to the bad choice, we have to set actual barriers to prevent bad decisions. Even adults must do this. For example, one particularly vulnerable place for me is the In-N-Out drive-through, upon receipt of my family's order. Six orders of salty, steaming-hot fries are supposed to sit beside me for ten minutes untouched? Not going to happen. After snacking on a few, I literally toss the bag onto the passenger floor. Because I know that despite reason and sound judgment, if I have the *option* to eat most of my children's fries, I will absolutely do it.

All human beings have the propensity to make bad choices despite good intentions. This is true for teenagers. You and I both can attest to this, because the results of my own comprehensive study (that I conducted right now in my head) show that a whopping 100 percent of adults were teenagers at some point. Also, science provides biological evidence that brains are not fully developed until we are twenty-five. Adults think with the rational part of the brain, while teens think with the emotional part.[7]

As parents, it's our job to set up boundaries to help our kids individually, based on their needs and inclinations. Your long-term plan involves creating boundaries that make sense for your children and your home.

Below is a list of ideas you can include to create your long-term plan. You can build this plan to be perfectly tailored to suit you and your kids. Pick and choose the parameters that you want to incorporate into your own plan, and ignore the ones that you don't like. Depending on your kids' ages and maturity, you will likely have different rules for each child. The hope would be that you give your children more freedom as you decide they are ready for it. You might start your fourteen-year-old with every rule in place, and by the time he is a senior, exactly no formalized rules remain. Great! Looks like you are preparing him to launch into adulthood, where he's responsible for his own decisions.

Phones remain docked in a specified location, not in children's pockets. Because we are using our phone as a helpful tool, like keys, wallets, and sunglasses, it will wait for us until we need to use it as a tool. We will pick it up when we need it, rather than having it beckon to us from our pockets with a buzz. When we leave the house, we will need our phone for GPS directions, for staying in contact with Mom and Dad, for connecting with friends we are meeting up with. Our kids can check their texts and other notifications during specifically designated times. Example: Before school they have fifteen minutes to respond to email, texts, and social media—after they are dressed and ready to go. After homework and before dinner, kids get thirty minutes to do the same, in the family room or kitchen, and then the phone returns to its docked location. You can create exact times and spaces that work best for you. The point is, you are creating discrete starting and stopping points for digital media.

Turn off all notifications for every app. If you have allowed social media and other apps for your children, they may check their notifications on your terms. Why should any random person who comments on a post have the power to pull your child from a family conversation or activity? They shouldn't. Your children will check notifications when it's best for your family. Simple as that. Kids do not need to be tapped on the shoulder all day long, beckoned away from real-life connection so that they can read every comment and see every like in real time. They understandably want to see if anyone reacted to their posts, and they will. Apps do not get to determine where we pay attention and when. We decide that. Turning off notifications helps with this.

No phones, tablets, or computers allowed in bedrooms. There is no reason for a young child to retreat to his bedroom alone with access to the entire world. A bedroom with a device is no longer a safe haven for a child. During the '80s and '90s, kids may have had phones and TVs in their rooms. But TV networks had standards and ratings. Anyone who wanted to call your child would need access to his phone number. Thanks to the Wild West of the internet, where anyone can stream anything, these protections are gone. Handing a child a device with unmitigated internet access is akin to our parents subscribing our bedroom TV sets to all pay-per-view channels. Not wise.

Phones may be used for texts and calls only. This is a great way to introduce your kids to the responsibility of living in a tech world. See how they handle this amount of personal technology, with the mutual understanding that it is a privilege and not a right. Mom or Dad may pick up the phone and check it at any time. You purchased your child's phone to help her connect to friends and family. How generous of you! If your child is having difficulty viewing this as generous and is instead complaining, you can remind her that you'd be happy to keep the phone for a while so that she can remember what life was like without the privilege you generously allowed.

No sending or receiving photos. Disabling the ability to send and receive photos removes the temptation for kids to send private photos in the first place. They might *say* that they don't like this, but internally, think of the relief. Even if they're peer pressured, our kids can blame their parents for the inability to do something that will later lead to regret. What parents wouldn't happily be an excuse for their child feeling pressured to make a terrible choice? How many stories have you heard of teen girls sending nude photos to an adolescent boyfriend, who forwards them to his entire football team or posts them online? The permanency of momentary indiscretion can't be overstated. Disabling photo messaging is a great course for kids who are still developing wisdom and self-control. Parents get the final say as to when kids can send and receive photos.

Cap social media, games, and other time-sucking apps at a chosen time limit. Install an app that will simply block access to chosen time-wasting activity once a time limit has been reached. If you've allowed thirty minutes per day for Instagram, once the time has been met, the app simply will not open.

Designate time windows and locations for parent-approved apps. You have decided that your daughter is ready for a social media account. She may access Instagram on the family desktop in the kitchen from 4:00 to 4:30. Or sitting with Mom or Dad as they look through her feed together.

Amy's fourteen-year-old daughter is allowed to have an Instagram account, but it is linked to Amy's. At any time, Amy can toggle between the accounts, checking direct messages, profiles, followers, and notifications.

Don't give your kids a data plan, and turn on Wi-Fi for select devices only during specified hours. We implemented this for every teenager who lived in our home through foster care. None had data plans on the phones they brought into our home. We provided them with our Wi-Fi password—but set time limits for each individual device through our router. At 6:00 pm, Wi-Fi access turned off. At around 6:03 the girls would inevitably show up in the kitchen, ready to hang out and chat. (There's your gentle parental nudge.) Create reasonable and loving barriers to tech overuse, and everyone will be grateful.

A great long-term plan will start with boundaries and barriers. As your kids grow in character and self-control, you can slowly eliminate some of them. You and your spouse can come to these decisions together while your child grows in wisdom and responsibility. By the time your child is a senior in high school, your goal is to move them toward almost no parentally imposed restrictions at all. But your kids are moving toward adulthood slowly. Your rules for tech will taper off gradually, like the launch scaffolding for a space shuttle. Picture a shuttle roaring into the sky. The poles that served a critical purpose prelaunch fall away after serving their purpose. But if they are removed too soon—or are never present to begin with—the rocket will never launch at all.

See the Recommended Reading list in the back for more resources on teens and tech.

"MY PARENTS SAVED ME"

We were enjoying dinner with friends when the conversation turned to the perennial discussion of nature versus nurture. As a mom to many, I was observing how unique each child is. "Our kids are all wired so differently from one another, it makes me think that parents have less ability to impact how our kids turn out than I initially thought," I said. My friend Cayla quietly listened and then smiled and shook her head.

"You know, anytime I hear parents say that—that they don't have the kind of impact they thought, I have to share my story, because I disagree. Parents have the power to change their kids' lives, even the unruliest kids. I know this, because I was a terrible child," she said, in her characteristically sweet Cayla voice. As soon as the words came out, I almost laughed because I didn't believe her. Cayla is a doting mother and selfless friend. We've served together in inner-city ministry. She has a degree in early childhood education and embraced screen-limited parenting much earlier than I did. I didn't believe she was a terrible kid because she's a phenomenal adult. She could see the doubt on my face.

"I'm serious!" She smiled. "When I was a teenager, I sneaked off and started dating a guy. My parents had no clue. This was before cell phones were widespread, so we had this notebook we would write in back and forth to each other. I'd hide it in the bushes near my house and he'd come and get it. He was bad news, and so was his dad. We talked about how they could help me get emancipated from my parents. We talked about running away together."

I couldn't believe what I was hearing.

"But then my parents found the notebook. They read the whole thing. They knew everything. And they took away every bit of privacy I had. They pulled me out of school and homeschooled me. They even took my bedroom door off its hinges! Of course I said I was mad at them. But internally I remember feeling a huge sense of relief that I didn't have to hide anymore. It was a full year before I began earning back the trust I had broken. Looking back, I am so, so grateful. I've thanked them over and over again. My parents saved me."

The story of forbidden teenage love isn't new. But the ease through which our kids can make terrible choices is. When we hand our kids a smartphone, we give them total accessibility without accountability.

I have lost count of the stories I've heard of kids using their phones to connect with peers and predators to make life-altering decisions. Drugs, sex, running away from home. I think about Cayla's parents often, encouraged by their commitment to fight for their daughter, even when she protested. While this tactic was exactly what Cayla needed, it may not be able to be generally applied to every single instance of teenage rebellion with equal success. But it highlights the importance of parental discernment and resolve. As parents, your attention to your kids and willingness to lovingly engage in ways that are individually tailored to their needs—that is powerful and life-changing. Remember, your kids do not have the long-game view that you do. Confidently create your plan and parameters based on your parental insight. Don't abandon your powerful role as parents when your kids need you most. The stakes are too high.

— 9 —

Great Uses for Screens:
Tech and Leisure

All technology has no conscience of its own. Whether it will become a force for good or ill depends on man.

JOHN F. KENNEDY

"MOM, CAN YOU PLAY THE SONG 'River of Grace' by
Christy Nockels?"

"Actually, sweetie, this is the radio and not my phone playing
the music, and I'm driving so I can't look at it right now," I explained to my four-year-old, who was accustomed to listening to
Mom's hand-selected playlist in the car. My phone's Bluetooth
wasn't connecting. "We have to listen to what's on the radio. We
can't pick the songs."

"Okay, well can you start this song over then?" Radio was a
difficult concept to explain to a child accustomed to on-demand
music. I tried again.

"No . . . it's the radio. I can't control anything about how the song plays. Someone else, the DJ, is choosing the music. You know, back when I was a kid, we'd have to call in to radio stations to request songs that we wanted to hear. I'd wait on hold forever to ask for the latest Britney Spears song, then wait another hour for the DJ to finally play it. I'd scramble to record it on a cassette tape so that I could listen to that song whenever I wanted. It was way different back then, huh?"

"Wow, that's weird. . . . Who is Britney Spears?"

So much has changed in the digital world over the past fifty years, it's hard to keep up. Remember when a Walkman and then Discman were high tech? Remember the sound of a landline's dial tone? (Note: If you're old enough to know what a dial tone sounds like, it's time for wrinkle cream.)

Fast-forward thirty years: Now we hear a snippet of a catchy new song at a store, use an app to identify what song is playing, and then add it to our digital library—all within fifteen seconds. Despite making me feel geriatric (my kids don't know who Britney Spears is?!), the advances in tech have served us well.

Remote working, personal DJ, online school. The same technology that enabled the globe to work and learn from home also revealed its own fundamental weakness: Man cannot live on screens alone. With anxiety and depression rates skyrocketing, it's clearer than ever that we need person-to-person connection. Technology can be helpful, but it cannot replace face-to-face time spent with real, live people.

Our children are spending one less hour socializing with friends face-to-face *per day* than millennials and Generation Xers did.[1] That's an hour less per day spent navigating emotions and relationships and negotiating boredom together. (These are pre-COVID-19 numbers!)

Nevertheless, a huge part of making your family's long-term plan is identifying the digital technologies that serve your family well. And there are certainly plenty. Your detox has no doubt clarified this for you. In this chapter, we will consider which types of screens you'd like to keep, and which you'd prefer to ditch.

First, we will explore the ways tech can serve your family as a tool and not as captor. By the time you finish thinking through all the great uses for tech in your everyday life, there will be no time left in your child's day for the life-wasting uses.

How to know what to keep and what to ditch

Ask yourself two questions:

1. Does this technology use help or hinder our family's long-term goals?
   If it helps, put the tech in its proper place. If it hinders, toss it.
2. Does this technology encourage isolated consumption of entertainment, with no clear long-term benefit?
   If yes, put it in its proper place, or toss it altogether.

For example, apply these considerations to the decision of whether to allow tablets, phones, or computers in the kids' bedrooms. Say your sixth grader enjoys using a device to call or text a friend. Your family's goals include helping your kids make and cultivate friendships. Sounds like a good use of tech as a tool! But once that helpful tool is moved into a bedroom, new hazards emerge. Internet-connected devices allowed in kids' bedrooms will motivate kids to stay in their bedrooms, alone, for hours. Does that further your family's goal to connect with each other? Or does it waste hours that could be spent cultivating skills and relationships? So determine that technology's proper place: in common areas of the home. Or make life simpler by replacing the tablet with a phone sans internet connection, and that can go into the bedroom for phone calls with friends.

Almost any technology we allow for our kids can be used well or foolishly. The best way to encourage wise use of these technologies is to walk closely alongside our kids as they begin to test the digital waters. We allow additional freedom little by little. A great kid can easily stumble into trouble online. At the same time, our kids' devices can be a useful tool for building friendships.

We want to capture the best parts of technology and teach our kids to do the same. What are some positive ways technology can be used well in the home? Next we will explore examples of technologies that can be used in great ways.

Your family may land in a slightly different place, and that's okay! You are tailoring your unique needs and interests to fit your kids. The important thing is that you are present, you are sifting, and you are showing your kids that screens are at their best when they are tools to spur real-life connection. Good job, Mom and Dad.

Helpful or neutral technologies for kids

Texting parents and friends. When kids are mature enough to stay home alone, they need a way to contact Mom or Dad. A home phone is perfect for this. Or maybe you've given your child a Gabb phone or other non-smartphone so that she can keep in contact with you when you are apart. (As discussed in chapter 7, I recommend waiting as long as possible to give your child a phone. If your child is not old enough to stay home alone for short spurts, she is likely too young for a phone.) Even without a phone, kids are still able to message Mom and Dad via Alexa or other voice-activated digital assistants. At some point, our kids grow into the age when they want to talk with friends after school. This is not new. We all remember holding our phone between our shoulder and our ear for hours as tweens. Create a way for your kids to connect with real humans and build friendships. Better yet, be the house that hosts the playdate or hangout. Remember, texting is a cheap substitute for rich communication. Help them cultivate the real-life stuff as much as you can.

Video calls. During the COVID-19 pandemic, we went from seeing grandparents weekly to never seeing them. FaceTime allowed us to catch up with Grandma and Grandpa. It's also a fun way for kids to see faraway cousins and family. Tweens enjoy texting and FaceTiming their buddies. This is a reality of growing up today. While we will not be giving our kids smartphones anytime soon, we do allow them to FaceTime their friends occasionally via Mom's phone, depending on their own maturity levels. At our kids' ages, FaceTime is done in the living room, kitchen, or bedroom with an open door.

Goodreads bookshelf. Our twelve-year-old daughter loves tracking the books she's read and wants to read through this helpful app. She may access her own account—on my phone or kitchen computer—whenever she finishes a book or wants to add a new one to her to-read shelf.

Library holds. My former doesn't-like-to-read son is now the most frequent requester of using the library app on my phone. He will reserve a few books at our local library and then periodically check his position on the waiting list. It also helps the kids manage their library accounts, which books are due back, etc.

Craft or cooking instructions. Your child wants to bake a chocolate chiffon cake, but your kitchen skills cap out at Duncan Hines. Enter YouTube baking channels. Take a few minutes to vet content. As I mentioned in chapter 6, supervision is everything. Keep the tablet or computer in the kitchen while your child surfs YouTube cooking pages.

Showing your kids the music, movies, etc. of your youth. "Hey, Siri, play Britney Spears," for example. (Although her lyrics sound quite different to my parent ears than they did to my sixteen-year-old ears. Most voice assistants have explicit-language filtering.) Have a blast watching *Star Wars*, *Lord of the Rings*, and all the

Disney classics of our youth. How fun to share the pop-culture icons of our childhood with our own children.

Check ratings and appropriateness of specific programs. In the unending world of digital media, parents cannot possibly vet every program for our growing kids. Thankfully, websites have done much of the vetting for us. PluggedIn.com is hosted by Focus on the Family. It reviews books, games, shows, movies, and YouTube channels. Start teaching your older kids how to vet the materials they are considering consuming. We teach them discernment when they are young and prayerfully allow them more and more freedom to make informed decisions as they grow older.

Family movie night. Enjoy the latest family flicks with your kids. Snuggle and make a list of favorite Christmas flicks to rewatch every year. Don't forget the popcorn.

Trivia night. Kahoot and Jackbox are two of our family's favorite online multiplayer games. Congregate in the family room like it's your own modern game show. Laughter guaranteed to ensue.

Digital home assistants. These handy little pods can serve as DJ, fact-checker, podcast broadcaster, audiobook narrator, and light-switch operator (like The Clapper of the twenty-first century). There are lots of ways a digital assistant can serve your family well. Ours reminds me of appointments and sets timers. There are kids' versions and music filters that can block explicit content. Parents can also review every voice command uttered to your digital assistant via your online account.

Audiobooks. One of our foster kids struggled to sit still for story time, every time. Her teacher approached me after school one day and told me that she found a classroom activity that enraptured her. This bouncy, distractable little lady would sit still as could be for the headphone audiobook station. Listening to the book through her headphones and then turning the pages with the chimes made our little girl feel so big. She couldn't get enough. Help improve your kids' listening comprehension by installing the Audible app on your digital home assistant, or check out audiobooks via the library. You can download them onto your phone in an instant and play the book from your car speakers on road trips. Like with read-aloud books, you develop family culture and story while you listen, rooting for the good guys and laughing together at the silliness.

Toothbrush timer apps. One simple, free app helped our kids brush their teeth so well, our dentist even noticed the vast improvement. The app includes a song, a selfie-type video, and a two-minute timer. At the end of the timer, kids get an opportunity to catch a prize. So for those two minutes, the kids are scrubbing their hearts out. My four-year-old scrubbed so vigorously that she would finish her turn with toothpaste foam in her hair and on her shirt, and with teeth so sparkly, I almost needed sunglasses. If your kids could use improvement on the brushing front, this app could prove a helpful tool.

Learning an instrument. Piano, guitar, tin whistle. Our own kids learned to play fun songs on the piano when in-person lessons weren't an option. Tech is at its best when it's used as a tool to learn a real-life skill. Take advantage of it!

Sort and sift

As you sift through home technologies, you are giving yourself the gift of clarity. This means that you won't have that uneasy feeling when your long-term plan does allow for a family movie or for your child to maintain a Goodreads account, to put library books on hold, or to watch an instructional video about origami.

I happen to love introducing my kids to preselected hilarious viral videos. Sometimes I'll share my iPhone screen to the living room TV, where I play cute animal compilations or funny songs. Or we'll learn new viral dance trends together. Enjoying appropriate content *together* is a fantastic use of screens. We are living in a digital world, and we should show our kids positive ways to use digital media. You will be sifting, categorizing, clarifying, and making plenty of mistakes along the way. (Getting it wrong is not a new aspect of parenting!) Sorting helps us gain confidence as parents, because we know that our technology plan is intentional and not haphazard.

Sift and categorize your home technologies: Is this video game or app digital kale or digital Skittles? Skittles are fine once in a while. But if you binge all day, you'll feel terrible. Your long-term plan is rooted in thoughtful consideration of your long-term parenting goals. As you show your children the ways you use technology as a tool—to cultivate skills, to connect with those we cannot see, and for assistance in the real world—they will follow your lead. Gone are the days of endless, mindless tech consumption.

As you make your long-term plan for your kids, remember the aspects of life you're trying to cultivate: face-to-face interactions and developing real-life skills. Tech that helps facilitate this is helpful. Tech that displaces it is not.

What about digital games and social media?

- Seventy-one percent of parents of a child under the age of twelve say they are "at least somewhat concerned their child might ever spend too much time in front of screens."[2]
- Seventy-one percent "believe the widespread use of smartphones by young children might potentially result in more harm than benefits."[3]
- Eighty-six percent of parents think their kids "spend too much time gaming."[4] (A majority of parents also believe that the amount of time their kids spend gaming is typical for other kids.)

It's time for parents to stop caring so much about "what is typical" and instead ask, "What is best?" There is absolutely a way for our kids to enjoy video games and social media without excessively using them at the expense of real-life activities. And it's our job to teach them how.

Video games

Time in simulation gets children ready for more time in simulation. Time with people teaches children how to be in relationship, beginning with the ability to have a conversation.[5]

We must consider what video-game play is displacing and what the games' content is communicating to our kids. To the first point, one study showed that teens who play video games regularly spent 30 percent less time reading than teens who didn't.[6] Reading increases kids' mental health and well-being.

As for content, if a video game contradicts the values you are working to impart, then allowing it would be self-defeating, not to mention confusing for your kids. Let's say you teach your twelve-year-old son that governing authorities are to be respected, that objectifying women is wrong, and that a life of crime is a path to jail. But then you allow him to play Grand Theft Auto. In this game, players take on the role of hardened criminals who premeditate crimes like killing police officers, civilians, and gang members, even requiring players to torture people in order to level up. Players do drugs and drink alcohol virtually. At one point in the game, a strip club scene allows avatars to fondle topless strippers.[7] "But, Dad! I can skip the strip club scene! Plus, all my friends are playing it!" your son objects. "Okay, fine . . . but only one hour per week," said no sane parent ever.

That said, just because many video games are terrible doesn't mean they all are. Check those ratings. Most kids over eight can play an appropriate video game with siblings or buddies for an hour once a week without slipping back into pre-detox haze. If your kids aren't asking for them, it's probably not worth initiating.

But if they are, we are wise to teach them how to enjoy occasionally, but not binge on this modern pastime.

Play alongside your kids, and let them see that what matters to them matters to you because you're their parent and because you want to enjoy their favorite things with them. Author and researcher Shaunti Feldhahn studied nearly three thousand teens. Ninety-four percent said they wished their parents actively worked to be involved with them. One child's example was to play video games with him, "especially when I know gaming isn't really my mom's thing!"[8] Sometimes, connecting with our kids can mean picking up a Nintendo controller.

I will never forget the time my mom visited me and my husband as newlyweds, and we all played Super Mario Bros. together. My mom was both highly competitive and extremely unskilled. She obliviously killed off her teammates and repeatedly lost the game for all of us. We nearly died of laughter.

If your family enjoys video games, there are thousands available to choose from. Research and vet the games that interest your kids. You can even use YouTube to watch others play a specific game to get a taste of it before you allow it. When you identify a few that are acceptable, play them with your kids. Video games, like all tech, are best enjoyed together. And with everything we know about the addictive component of video games, we are mindful that even those with harmless content can hinder our family's goals when played excessively or alone. If each child has one or two hours of total free time per day, what percentage of that time do you want video gaming to comprise? Remember, the time our children have available to cultivate interests, skills, relationships, and even to *think* is limited. Filling their free time with digital entertainment prevents them from accomplishing and enjoying the critical building blocks of childhood.

You used your digital detox to help cultivate your child's real-life skills, interests, and relationships. After your detox, there is no magical formula for the exact number of minutes your child should be spending in front of a screen. But the research shows: Less is better.

My three oldest children were former video game aficionados. After a lengthy detox and long-term plan that severely limited gaming, my ten-year-old son came in from playing lightsaber training with his siblings for three hours. "This is way more fun than video games," he said.

If you'd told me pre-detox that this child would play with sticks for three hours and then describe the experience as "way more fun than video games," there's no way I'd have believed you. But this is what happens when we rewire our kids' brains by nudging them toward creating, playing, and going outside.

Social media

"Social media is destroying our lives." . . . "So why don't you go off it?" I asked. "Because then we would have no life."[9]

As we discussed last chapter, kids under thirteen should not have social media, period. Even after thirteen, parents must seriously consider whether they want to expose their young kids to the type of mature and unfiltered content they will encounter online. When we allow our young kids on social media, aside from consuming questionable content, they instantly feel the pressure to create an online persona worth "liking." They curate a heavily filtered feed, spending an inordinate amount of mental and emotional energy projecting visual perfection. In generations past, adolescence was the time for kids to do the quiet, angsty, and awkward work of understanding how they are wired and their place in this big world. Social media interrupts this, burying our kids in a stream of outside influencers.

Too often, parents allow young kids on social media before the kids have had the opportunity to do the internal searching, the critical work of growing up. Instead of internal work, our kids are carefully crafting external highlight reels, more focused on the persona they are projecting to their peers and how they're being perceived. The sense of self is underdeveloped as kids are catapulted into the cutthroat land of performance and comparison. The American Psychological Association reports that "chronic attention to physical appearance leaves fewer cognitive resources available for other mental and physical activities."[10] What unnecessary stress to allow our kids to bear.

Instead, we want those formative years—the transition from child to adult—to be a time when our kids' primary influence is parents who love their kids madly, regardless of likes, followers, morning breath, acne, and bad hair days. The same way God loves us. Parents have the joy of representing unconditional love to our kids. This is the opposite of social media culture: conditional, judgmental, and superficial.

Still, there are dozens of ways social media *can* serve us well! Pastors frequently share biblically informed perspectives and counsel on current cultural events. Social media helps highly niched groups of people connect with one another. Never before could underwater basket weavers connect so easily with their people. Now, a simple search allows immediate connection. How cool is that?

In a climate where online bullying is at an all-time high, our kids have opportunities to reach out to hurting friends or lonely kids at school, encouraging them with positivity and kindness. They can check in with classmates who look sad or express concerning thoughts online.

You needn't scroll far online to find a message that reeks of logical fallacy or counter-productive thinking. We parents have the privilege of helping our kids learn to spot these and understand why they are incorrect. What is the right way to kindly and respectfully disagree with another human? When do we engage, when do we keep scrolling? These are critical lessons for today's kids, and a unique hurdle to our generation of parents. But we need not wring our hands. The same technology that is rife with parental challenges also connects us with each other and with resources that speak into our concerns.

Before you allow your child to have a social media account, I highly recommend that both of you read *The Teen's Guide to Social Media and Mobile Devices* by Jonathan McKee. McKee explores and contextualizes the content kids will encounter online, while equipping them with common-sense tools.

For parents: If you want to read more about the current landscape in tweens, teens, and social media, *American Girls: Social Media and the Secret Lives of Teenagers* by Nancy Jo Sales is an eye-opening account from a secular perspective. The book provides data, anecdotes, and a general context for how the social media landscape has transformed adolescence from our own youth.

Tech tools for the Christian parent

Imagine you teleported Paul of Tarsus to the present day. You show him bookshelves full of bound and printed Bibles, commentaries, and written collections from the wisest preachers in history. (You may take a moment to fill Paul in on the glorious, world-changing printing press.) Then you pull your phone from your pocket to show Paul the internet, that every Scripture is accessible within seconds—in nearly every language. For free.

And get this, Paul: Unlike in first-century Judah, 80 percent of American adults can understand the words on the pages in front of them.[11] Those who can't read can listen to any Bible translation, any sermon, or any Scripture passage set to music. The availability of biblical resources and the capability to understand them is more promising than in any time in history. I bet Paul would be so excited, that thorn in his side would feel more like a feather.

There are many excellent resources online for our kids. Often, we simply need a fellow parent to vet them and tell us which are worth our time. I've sifted through many resources for you. Here are a few I've found to be the most useful.

- Music artist and dad Ross King, also known as **King Things**, has created helpful tools for families to memorize enormous chunks of Scripture in a fun and pleasant way. As a mom who did not grow up memorizing Scripture, I have cherished doing so alongside my kids now. There is no way I'd have as much fun committing Genesis 1 to memory without King Things's beautiful song. His music is pleasant and pretty, not like some of the bubble-gummy Christian music that makes your ears cry. Find King Things on Amazon, YouTube, and more.

- **New City Catechism** (NCC) is a system of simple questions and answers to basic theological questions. Example: "What is God?" "God is the creator of everyone and everything." There are fifty-two questions and answers like this that lay out the foundation of our faith and Christian beliefs. Rote memorization can feel like a chore, but NCC has developed an app and a song for each catechism question and answer. Play these in your car, and before you know it, your five-year-olds will be singing, "What hope does everlasting life hold for us? That we will live with and enjoy God forever in the new heaven and the new earth, where we will be forever freed from all sin in a renewed, restored creation." Music to a parent's ears (and, admittedly, more lyrically redemptive than Britney Spears). Find it at NewCityCatechism .com.

- **The Bible Project** produces free videos recapping the stories of the Bible in an educational and clear way. You can watch videos based on books or themes of the Bible. They offer podcasts, blogs, and classes to help people better understand God's Word and their place in his story. I highly recommend

watching these short videos with your kids. See BibleProject
.com.

Not that it's the most critical piece here, but one perk about the
resources listed above is that kids *and* adults enjoy them.

Family technology inventory

Take a moment to list a few technologies that serve your family
well. Write down specific technologies that have helped your people
connect with each other and create. Be specific. For example, "Computer" won't help you clarify much. The same machine that plays
Bible videos is also a gateway to porn. You want to create clear
parameters for tech that help you to further your family's long-term
goals. You want to stay away from consuming in isolation. Allowing
kids to use the kitchen computer to create a birthday wish list on
Amazon, print out a coloring page, or learn a new dance routine
could all be great items to list. Every family has slightly different
goals, interests, and home setup. Listing a few is going to help remind you how helpful technology can be, when it's in its right place.

Here is a clarifying tool to help you sort the technology in your
home. I've included examples, but this will look different for every
family, depending on kids' ages and interests.

**Green light tech: Specific uses that are almost always
okay**

- Examples: using a Word document to write stories at the
  kitchen computer, texting friends, requesting music from a
  digital assistant, placing library books on hold

**Yellow light tech: Ask Dad or Mom before using, or
refer to predetermined time rules**

- Examples: weekly Mario Kart, group game of trivia

Red light tech: For now, our kids will not be using these technologies, period

- Examples: social media, internet-connected devices in bedrooms, games or movies that contradict your family's values.

You can, of course, tape a list of allowable tech and accompanying tech rules to your fridge. In many situations, like with the most addictive forms of tech (social media, gaming), this can be helpful. If the kids know that they get only one hour of video gaming each week, it helps set expectations.

But we have found that most of our parenting and tech decisions happen on the fly, in the busy scurry of dishes and schoolwork. "Mom! Can I FaceTime my friend?" "Can we watch the football game?" "Can I Google how to get out of quicksand?" These sorts of requests happen at random and require parents to sift. It's helpful to have forethought about which tech is off the table (violent games, aimless YouTube surfing), which is enjoyed sometimes (hilarious viral videos pre-vetted by parents), and which we pretty much always say yes to (chess online with faraway cousins, Kindle use). As your kids mature, the types of tech you allow will graduate from red to yellow, and ultimately to green. It's the normal decision-making power transition from parent to child.

The most critical and freeing approach for moms and dads is to develop a *posture* toward tech consumption in your home. For example, after a lengthy exploration of the merits of eating processed foods, Michael Pollan famously summed up his posture toward food as simply this:

Eat food.

Not too much.

Mostly plants.[12]

Similarly, our tech posture as parents could be this:

Enjoy technology.
As a tool to enhance life.
Not supplant it.

Tech can be great. It can also displace the most important parts of life. So we rely on our posture as we move forward, sifting whatever new tech comes our way. You might find that though initially painful, the very process of deciding which tech to allow and disallow turns out to be its own gift. That's because you're teaching your kids how to apply your guiding principles to your decision-making process. You're showing them that you love them enough to roll up your sleeves and get in the weeds with them. Of course, this is seen easily in retrospect. While *in* the weeds, the struggle can make parents want to pull their hair out. Take heart. Your time and investment in your kids is worth it, even when you want to hide in the pantry and cry into a box of Cheez-Its.

Our long-term hope for our kids is that they launch into the world with strong character and the tools they need to make great decisions. They won't get there if they don't practice making decisions with our guidance and explanation for how we arrived at our own. Our rules are the scaffolding as we help them build a house of virtue.

Again, all families will differ a little on the finer points of their long-term plans. But those plans are built on the foundational truths and guiding principles Mom and Dad have established. For example, in our family, that means explaining that our lives are on loan to us from God. He gave us the breath in our lungs and loves the junk out of us. He tells us to love him and love our neighbors, so that's what we do. While there is no mention of Snapchat, Call of Duty, or Netflix in our Bibles, we know there is nothing new under the sun. Diversions have been around since

Eve couldn't stop staring at that fruit, lured into a decision that caused generational demise. We meet these decision crossroads every day—choosing, sifting, considering.

However you create your long-term plan, you will do so remembering that it is our joy and duty as parents to show our kids how to appreciate but not binge on the best the world has to offer. We must protect our kids from the poisonous effects of too much and the wrong kind of tech. We do this humbly, knowing we will get it wrong sometimes. But we are always reassessing our kids' needs and readjusting the way we shepherd them. We do this from the bedrock of relationship and love, teaching them how to pursue wisdom and exercise virtue.

—— 10 ——

Tech and Learning

What students were willing to do, what they were capable of doing in 2010, versus today . . . it shocks me to my core. Diminished attention spans, anxiety through the roof. . . .

LAUREN, AP HISTORY TEACHER

Too much screen time too soon is the very thing impeding the development of the abilities that parents are so eager to foster through the tablets.

DR. ARIC SIGMAN

IN A COMMERCIAL BREAK during the 2010 Academy Awards, Apple announced it was launching a shiny new device, certain to improve our lives: the iPad. The tablet was billed as a tool to read the *New York Times* (sophisticated!), check your investment portfolio (wealthy!), read the latest bestseller (smart!). An entire generation couldn't wait to get their hands on it, a symbol of luxury and technical prowess. Soon enough, apps for the littlest kids to learn their ABCs sprang to the marketplace. Fancy *and* educational?! We were sold. I bought a special case for our iPad so that our kids could tap away without scratching. I prided myself on creating future rocket scientists.

Twelve years later, we wish we'd never started. Teachers tell us our kids have more trouble paying attention than generations before. Put bluntly, we were duped.

What our kids really need to develop is sustained attention, impulse control, and active listening. Screens cultivate the opposite. Somehow, slick marketing convinced us we were educating our kids when we were just entertaining them. Of course, kids love the dopamine squirts and novelty of digital candy. And to be honest, parents love the break it provides. If the kids love it, how can it be bad? So the tech-ed industry is booming, with many school districts spending billions to put a tablet in every backpack. Before carefully considering if flooding classrooms with digital media is best, we are drinking the advertising Kool-Aid and calling it advancement.

Tablets for everyone

"Mom, we get free tablets! Every kid at school gets one! They're educational," my kids said. We were a year post-detox at this point. Our iPads had been gathering dust. But now the school was giving away tablets for free, under the guise of education. I was equal parts dubious and curious. To the school library we went. Sure enough, the librarian handed me three brand-new tablets preloaded with "educational apps."

"Okay, guys. Dad and I will charge these and see what's on them. We'll let you know if and how you're allowed to use them." My husband and I scrolled through the tablets to find song-based infant-type tapping games. Hardly the stuff worth our kids' time. We deleted every app except Kindle. The kids prefer hard copies of books, so it didn't take long before the tablets were tucked into a cupboard, forgotten.

We began receiving emails from the school district: "Is everything okay? Your child's tablet has not connected to our servers in more than thirty days." If we hadn't detoxed our kids already, if I hadn't read the studies and books that showed me time and time again that tablets cause more harm than good for our kids, I would have absolutely let our kids play on them. I'd have felt proud, even, as they tapped away. "Free tech device that helps my kids learn? The school is providing it, so it must be beneficial!"

But I couldn't unsee what I saw after we detoxed our kids. I couldn't unknow what I had learned after reading dozens of books and studies and talking to teachers, education experts, and doctors.

Steve Jobs once believed that technology in classrooms was the golden ticket to fixing education, until he realized it wasn't. "I've probably spearheaded giving away more computer equipment to schools than anybody on the planet. But . . . what's wrong with education cannot be fixed with technology."[1]

Education psychologist Dr. Jane Healy also expected tech would help fix what's broken in education. After years of research, she discovered that her initial assumption was wrong. "Time on the computer might interfere with development of everything from the young child's motor skills to his or her ability to think logically."[2]

Harvard Law School professor Carol Steiker is a convert to low-tech classroom approaches. After allowing note-taking via laptops in her classes, she noticed that students who did so suffered from inattention to the lessons. Why? Note-taking on laptops changed the nature of learning. Instead of listening, thinking, and organizing thoughts, students were self-appointed transcribing machines. She initially banned laptops, but noticed the students were still distracted by their smartphones. Steiker now allows no technology in any of her classes.[3]

Victoria Prooday, an occupational therapist, has observed,

> After hours of virtual reality, processing information in a classroom
> becomes increasingly challenging for our kids because their brains

are getting used to the high levels of stimulation that video games provide. The inability to process lower levels of stimulation leaves kids vulnerable to academic challenges.[4]

Our kids are continually overstimulated. Then we expect them to throttle down and focus on a typical lecture, and they can't. These are normal kids who are responding appropriately to a stimulus. They aren't deficient in something if they have trouble focusing on a hum-drum math lesson when they've been conditioned to crush candy while Netflix-bingeing. Adults aren't immune to overstimulation impairment. Try watching a Michael Bay film while scrolling social media for two hours. After that, pick up a Jane Austen novel. You will find it difficult to focus on something that requires sustained attention. No need for us to feel prideful or prejudiced about attentional vulnerabilities; that's simply how the human brain works. We must practice the skills we want to build.

Myth busters, tech-and-learning edition

The marketing machine is busy at work, using our kids against us. How do we know what's true about the way tablets, smartphones, and games impact our kids' abilities to learn? Let's sift through the smoke and mirrors.

Myth: Tablets and virtual games are a great way for toddlers to learn educational skills they need

Infants and toddlers cannot retain and learn from digital media in the same way that they learn from their parents. Studies have shown that small children aren't able to transfer digital knowledge into the real world.

Speech therapist Monica Gomez told me, "Parents come to my office saying, 'My child has fifty words!' Their three-year-old will be spouting out words, 'bird,' 'tree,' 'apple,' but after a few minutes it becomes clear—it's not functional language they're learning. They don't know what those words correspond to. The child is parroting sounds they hear from apps, games, and tablets. When kids learn words this way, their learning doesn't translate into the real world."[5]

Most apps parents find under the "educational" category in app stores have no evidence of efficacy and use little or no input from educators or developmental specialists. According to medical experts, the best way for youngest children to learn anything from digital media is for parents to watch alongside their kids, and then reteach the same lesson in person.[6] At that point, why not cut out the middleman? Our smallest kids need hands-on play and conversation with a loving adult to develop their cognitive skills, verbal skills, fine and gross motor skills, and social-emotional skills. Read a book, take a walk, make letters out of Play-Doh.

Babies do not learn language effectively from iPads. They learn best from a loving caregiver. Despite what advertisers say, tablets and videos do not support language development in the way parents hope—or in the way marketing campaigns would like us to believe. A recent study showed that kids who use more screen time at two and three years old performed worse on developmental screenings at ages three and five.[7]

That "rapt-attention" face on your small child is the look of overstimulation, not of learning. Parts of an infant's brain only respond to real people who are present and attentive. This has shown to be especially true when those "real people" are doting parents the baby already knows and loves.[8]

I interviewed Joe Clement, a twenty-seven-year teacher, author, and parent, and asked him what he thought about parents using digital devices for their kids' educational advancement. He said, "Too many parents are blindly buying into marketing campaigns that say, 'This is the twenty-first century. Kids need twenty-first-century skills. . . .' The irony is that kids need to be able to do the skills that are *harmed* by screens. Those things that make us human are never going away."[9]

Myth: Kids need the digital efficiency to keep up with the rigorous demands of today

Despite parents repeating to each other that "kids have so much more homework these days than we did as kids," the data simply doesn't bear that out. A data study that surveyed 11 million people showed that the current crop of eighth, tenth, and twelfth graders spent less time on homework than Gen X teens did in the early 1990s. In fact, students today are spending less time on homework, paid work, volunteering, and extracurriculars *combined*, not more.[10]

Matt Miles, a high school teacher, author, and parent, told me that students and parents often complain that an assignment "takes hours." "It's a twenty-minute assignment. But the student's attention is divided, so it takes them 'hours' to complete it."[11]

Our kids don't need costly digital gadgets to keep up with the world around them. They need parents who are willing to roll up their sleeves and be honest with them, despite protests.

Myth: Multitasking is how kids learn these days

Multitasking degrades—not enhances—productivity and learning. Clifford Nass, a psychology professor at Stanford University, says that multitasking wastes more time than it saves and damages concentration and creativity. Nass says the difference between people who multitask and those who do not are remarkable. "People who multitask all the time can't filter out irrelevancy. They can't manage a working memory. They're chronically distracted. They initiate much larger parts of their brain that are irrelevant to the task at hand. . . . They're even terrible at multitasking. When we ask them to multitask, they're actually worse at it. So they're pretty much mental wrecks."[12]

What can parents do with this information?

Cultivate deep thought and sustained focus in your kids. Say no to frenetic, rapid toggling.

Myth: Earlier access to electronics best equips kids for the future in our digital world

Katie claims her son Aiden is a "computer genius," because he will use the iPad for three consecutive hours. "He can figure out how to do anything on there! He is naturally great at computers." What's more likely, and bad news for Katie, is that her son is entertaining himself on a screen that has been engineered to function very easily for any human, including those with the lowest IQs. To pretend that a child who loves his iPad is necessarily computer savvy is like saying your child has a chef's palate because he likes eating potato chips.

Google executive and Dartmouth alum Alan Eagle addresses this myth directly: "At Google and all these places, we make technology as brain-dead easy to use as possible. There's no reason why kids can't figure it out when they get older."[13]

What kids really need is to develop and master fundamental skills before they have digital tools. Otherwise, they rely on the tools instead of their skills, becoming enslaved to their digital devices.

Think about the technology that was around when you were five. I'm picturing Teddy Ruxpin and Speak & Spell. Did the technology of the 1980s prepare your five-year-old self for the future tech-driven workforce? If I told you I took a course on "How to be proficient in America Online" in 1996, we would all laugh about that having been a huge waste of time. Technology changes rapidly, and our kids are much better equipped for those changes by honing their critical-thinking and problem-solving skills than by playing with a technology that will be laughably obsolete by the time they finish high school.

174

The hard truth is that earlier access to electronics simply trains our kids to be entertained nonstop. Kids are not using digital media to learn and create; they're using it to veg. Young people only spend about 3 percent of their digital time on content creation.[14] When a young life is spent being digitally entertained for hours each week, for years, what happens when that child reaches adulthood?

Let's look at the recent crop of adults who came of age in the screen-entertainment zone. In 2016, approximately one in four non-college-educated men in their twenties had not worked in the past year. Men in their twenties used to be the most reliably employed of all demographic groups. What happened? University of Chicago economist Erik Hurst found that instead of working or going to school, the men in this demographic are playing video games. "The life of these nonworking, lower-skilled young men looks like what my son wishes his life was like now: not in school, not at work, and lots of video games."[15]

Kids who start early with tech entertainment are training themselves for a future of being entertained by screens.

Myth: Parents and teachers should keep kids entertained to engage their learning abilities

Do we really want to condition our kids to be entertained in order for them to pay attention to an activity? Do we want them to expect the real world to be a cruise ship?

Let's say, for the sake of argument, that we didn't mind entertaining our kids if it was an effective method of teaching. Here's the only problem: There's little proof that digital-entertainment-based learning works.[16] But that hasn't dampened marketing efforts.

In our entertain-me digital world, video game companies have attempted to capitalize by marketing their products as educational. Parents of distractable gamers may initially think this is a fabulous idea. Unfortunately, studies have shown information learned through gaming is not retained effectively. This is because our kids' motivation in gaming is not learning but scoring points.[17]

How do teachers feel about this?

"They're having to dumb down everything in order to step down into the kids' simplified digital existence. Rather than deal with the issues created by technology addiction, schools are trying to trick digital natives into learning by sneaking small, palatable doses of education into their games and social media," said teachers Joe Clement and Matt Miles.[18]

Aric Sigman, an associate fellow of the British Psychological Society and a fellow of Britain's Royal Society of Medicine, says, "When very small children get hooked on tablets and smartphones, they can unintentionally cause permanent damage to their still-developing brains. Too much screen time too soon is the very thing impeding the development of the abilities that parents are so eager to foster through the tablets. The ability to focus, to concentrate, to lend attention, to sense other people's attitudes and communicate with them, to build a large vocabulary—all those abilities are harmed."[19]

The truth is that people do their best thinking when their mind is inactive. Participants in one study produced creative and higher-quality ideas while simultaneously engaged in a boring activity.[20] (Maybe that's why your most inspiring ideas hit you in the shower!) It turns out that inundating and overloading the senses with stimuli doesn't help anyone think better.

Myth: Technology has no place in education

"My daughter enjoys computer coding and even takes special classes. Isn't that a good use of technology?"

This *can be* a great use of technology. My kids have also enjoyed coding and programming classes. Take a moment to clarify what you want the purpose to be. If your child is using the coding program mostly to play games other people have created, that's probably not a great use of time. If she's spending all her free time in front of a computer, you'll likely want to adjust that. Assess and decide with intention: How much of your child's life do you want tech to consume? Then create daily parameters and habits that further your plan, and stick to it.

As I pen this manuscript, my kids' school is primarily online, due to county-mandated school shutdowns. Thanks to incredible teachers and an option of hybrid online and in-person learning, my kids have been mostly appreciative of the setup, although it didn't take long for them to begin to express disdain for sitting in front of a computer screen all day. Many have been grateful for the option to learn online when physical learning was not an option. That said, the COVID-19 distance-learning explosion shone a spotlight on the elephant in the room: Full-time virtual learning for kids is tremendously deficient. Kids learn best with face-to-face socialization with peers and teachers. With wide-scale online learning, kids are more depressed, less able to focus, and falling behind academically. In-person learning is preferable.

Digital tools can enhance our kids' learning. But technology should only be used when it's the best option available. It should also be used sparingly. If we honestly pursue the former, the latter inevitably follows.

How: Parents can fix what's broken, and it starts in the home

So what can parents do now to best help their kids succeed, in spite of tech overuse in schools?

Clarify as parents what you want your kids to value. I interviewed Lauren, a teacher at a high-performing high school in Southern California, and asked her about the current learning climate. She told me her students are more anxious than ever before. They don't care about learning—they only want the A.

Everything hinges on their ability to get into an Ivy league school. It's the social currency of their world.

"Do you think that parents never stopped to ponder, 'What do we want to cultivate in this child; what truly makes for successful parenting?'" I asked her. "In the absence of a thoughtful answer to this question, have parents decided that their own success hinges on the ranking of their kids' colleges?"

"Absolutely," she replied. "Kids are stressed out, and they can't think critically. Parents are combative about grades. . . . Where's the virtue? Where's the sense of duty? Where's ethical and moral principles? I don't see it."[21]

Parents are humans. Humans like metrics. If we don't clarify our metrics, culture will autofill for us. Most parents don't stare at their one-year-old and think, *Help me, Harvard-bound one, you're my only hope.* And yet many of us fall into the rat race anyway. In the absence of clearly defined purpose, we get autofilled parenting.

The takeaway? Clarify your purpose and guiding principles as parents. You did this at the end of chapter 1. Sift your parenting decisions through this.

Cultivate impulse control, deep thinking, and sustained attention in your kids. "Becoming indistractable is *the* most important skill for the 21st century—and it's one that many parents fail to teach their kids,"[22] says Stanford psychology expert Nir Eyal. Interestingly, the man who said this also wrote the bestselling book that app and video game designers have used to *create* addictive technology.

Parents today must work harder than previous generations of parents to cultivate the same attention skills that kids have always needed. We must start when they are tiny. Teach them the art of paying attention, even when the content is boring. How can our kids learn difficult concepts if they cannot focus long enough to process them? Dad and Mom are the best people to help build their children's focus, little by little. Reading books aloud and asking questions is one of the simplest and most effective ways to cultivate these skills. Excessive screen use will undermine these efforts.

Teach kids how to converse respectfully and how to disagree well. We want to raise kids who can politely listen and converse even when it's not fun, like when Grandma retells the story about walking to school, in the snow, uphill, both ways—for the fifteenth time. Can your kids respectfully maintain eye contact and resist the urge to check out? We live in a world where loving your neighbor is often as simple as putting your phone away and giving them your full attention.

Dr. Leonard Sax recommends a simple and practical way to help create spaces for this: Maintain a no-headphones-in-the-car rule. "When you're in the car, you should be listening to your child, and your child should be listening to you—not to Cardi B or Billie Eilish."[23] Dr. Sax's point is a good one. Car rides are the perfect time to hone the art of conversation.

If you are going to use drive time to listen to music instead of chat, listen together. Technology that is used to connect is technology used well. As your kids grow older, they'll begin sharing their favorites with you. I will never forget showing my dad the cool songs of my day. "Dad, meet Snoop Dogg." Soon after, my fifty-year-old sweater-vest-clad father was telling people to drop things like they were hot.

Teach them the give-and-take of conversation over topics that are fun and low stakes.

Stop texting your kids when they are in school. Don't let your child's phone become a mechanism for you to helicopter parent. We train our kids at home so they can work out their own problems at school. When we virtually tap our kids on the shoulder all day, they miss opportunities to navigate and troubleshoot in their own world. Recess and lunch are precious minutes for our kids to spend socializing with friends. We don't want to pull them away from that. As teacher Joe Clement said during our interview, it's time for parents to "cut the digital umbilical cord."

Make your expectations clear to your kids for when phone use is acceptable at school. A huge problem for teachers is that kids are entertaining themselves on their phones during class time. This disrespects the teacher and cripples our kids' ability to learn the material they need.

Several teachers have told me they have simply stopped taking kids' phones away during class, even though they're distracting students. Why? "We don't have parental support," one teacher told me. Parents can support teachers by training their kids that phones are not to be touched during class.

Nudge your kids toward screen-free educational options when available. People generally retain more of what they read when they read from a real book, as opposed to an electronic device. Digital devices present a slew of distractions a click away, discouraging kids from deep, focused reading. When the school offers digital curriculum, ask if a hard copy is available.

I asked nationally recognized elementary school principal George Petersen how parents and schools can create the best learning environment for kids. "Children are designed to be nurtured and mentored by parents, teachers, and peers. To cultivate a child's most important attributes (social, emotional, verbal, and physical), children need to play and academically collaborate with their friends. Meaningful relationships with people help children grow into the best version of themselves."[24]

Talk to your kids. A lot. Experts agree that loving words from a parent is the golden ticket for our kids' brain growth and cultivating their educational potential. Talking to our kids when they are infants and toddlers is critically important, because it is such a vitally active language-learning window for their brains. The more words, the more back-and-forth conversation from a loving parent, the better off our kids will be.

When you run out of cool, funny, or even coherent words (we've all had those days), read aloud from your home or public library. Build vocabularies, connect, help develop delayed gratification and attention spans. The benefits go on. In contrast, screen time reduces talk time between parent and child.

Ask your teachers and schools about the role technology plays in the classroom. Ask teachers if they've noticed a decline in attention spans, empathy, impulse control. Share some of what you've been reading with them.

Bottom line

Studies show that less is best when it comes to our kids' use of tech in learning. Parents don't need to approach the tech-in-ed crisis with resigned shrugs. You are in the driver's seat. The battle might be uphill, but your kids are worth it. Yes, there can be some great ways to use technology as a tool in learning as kids get older. But the medical experts, teachers, and tech giants agree—wait longer to introduce technology to your kids.

Help your kids hone the fundamental skills of real-life person-to-person connection. Help them learn to take responsibility, make conversation, read real books, write with a pencil, problem-solve. The primary ingredient required in developing these fundamental skills? A present, loving parent.

Let's protect our kids, heeding the advice of experts and our common sense. The marketing experts don't care about our kids' long-term development. We do. Most non-Amish families decide that technology can have a role in education. But let's make those decisions with information and caution, appreciating our kids' vulnerabilities and the opportunity costs along the way.

— 11 —

A Detox and Long-Term Plan for Every Kind of Family

If rapid measures aren't taken, we may be in for serious problems. . . . It's no exaggeration to say that kids today are being controlled by smartphones and becoming enslaved by them.

RYUTA KAWASHIMA, NEUROSCIENTIST

NO TWO FAMILIES ARE THE SAME. Every detox and long-term plan will have unique needs and quirks. Every detox and long-term plan has hiccups. Exactly none are without friction. Some may be concerned that because of a specific facet of their family, a detox will not be an option for them.

Welcome to myth busters. I'm your host and I would officially like to bust this myth.

Every family can implement a digital detox and sustain their results with a new long-term plan. Working parents, single parents, foster parents, homeschool parents, parents with one child, parents with lots of children. You don't need a different family; you just need a willing heart, some determination, and a good attitude.

No matter what your family situation is like, you can implement a successful detox and long-term plan. You can UNDO the tech trance so that the digital devices are serving you and your kids, instead of the other way around. In this chapter, I will show you how.

Working parents

Of the families I have helped digitally detox their kids, the parents who have expressed the most pre-detox stress are dual-working households. I can't blame them, and can relate to the struggle through personal experience.

As I pen this book, my husband and I are both working and juggling six kids' distance-learning schedules. We maintain a strict tech diet for our kids. How? As much as I can, I work in the early morning, before our kids rise. We use babysitters and generous grandparents twice per week, for three to four-hour chunks. The benefits of keeping our kids from screens is worth paying a babysitter. When I must work alongside our chatty preschooler, I have a cupboard full of fun, creative, mind-building diversions: age-appropriate LEGO, Lincoln Logs, puzzles, paper and crayons, a matching game, and hard dinosaur eggs that you can etch away at with a tool, revealing treasures inside. Before hopping on a call or responding to an email, I sit with my preschooler for five to fifteen minutes, getting him started on one of these fun activities. Once he has the hang of it, I pivot to the work that requires my attention. This process is not always without frustration! But it is easier than I thought it would be pre-detox, and either way, it's worth it.

What if my job doesn't have this kind of flexibility?

Parents John and Tacie work from home, full-time. Their first attempt at digitally detoxing their two daughters failed within a few hours, when Mom found herself in a hostage-negotiation situation: She could either give in to the children wailing for iPads, or embarrass herself on a conference call with clients. Instead of risking her job, she handed over the iPads.

A few weeks later, she and her husband tried again, with new resolve. Mom knew she was more likely to give in to iPad requests than Dad, so she asked her husband to lock the tablets in a safe to help her stick to her plan. She did whatever it took to help her stick to their goals.

On the first day of detox attempt number two, the older daughter was relieved to have a break. But younger daughter? Not so much. "She cried for hours nonstop." No wonder Mom was stressed! Tacie stayed committed to the family's detox, despite her daughters' protests and setbacks.

After one week, I checked in with Tacie. Were the kids faring better the second time around? Did anybody get fired? Quite the opposite. The girls had stopped asking for the iPad altogether.

"It's a miracle!" she said. "Once a week goes by, it seems to click. Kind of like that 'three-day potty training,'" she said. An apt analogy. Remember that first day of potty training your two- or three-year-old? The beginning was a mess, a diaper storm of epically stinky proportions. But through sheer parental resolve, the concept finally clicks for your kids. They *will* get it. Some sooner, some later. And when they do, you will see that it has been worth all the hard work it took to get there.

Work-from-home mom Marissa has found it particularly helpful to create time blocks for her four kids during her workday. If she allowed her kids to play anywhere with an open schedule, they would often argue or get bored. Instead, she explains to her kids that they will spend thirty minutes in the playroom, followed by thirty minutes outside, and then lunch. Her kids play longer and more cooperatively with a blocked schedule. If an ornery child instigates conflict, Marissa removes the offender and has them quietly read beside her in the home office.

Here are some additional ideas and tips for working households, including feedback from other parents' experiences:

- Don't forget about your list. The same list of activity ideas you made before starting your detox can help you moving forward, into the long-term plan. Especially when kids claim to be dying of boredom.
- Hands-on, tactile activities are the most engaging. Kinetic sand, science experiments, board games, choreographing dance routines. Make a giant batch of homemade playdough like our moms did when we were kids. You will be surprised how long children of all ages will play with fresh playdough. I'm talking hours. That squish factor is hard to resist.
- Don't feel the need to make every activity an inherently fun one. Productivity can be its own reward. Don't assume that just because an activity helps the household, your kids will hate it. Tacie had her girls organize the books on their shelves, create a list of the book series they have, and track which specific books were missing. Her girls stayed busy with this task and enjoyed the sense of productivity. There are dozens of helpful tasks like this one, waiting for you to assign to your kiddos. Use your detox window to teach your kids how rewarding it is to accomplish a productive household task. We are all wired for work. Tap into this innate desire in your kids, looking out for the kind of work they are particularly good at. They will not like it at first, but push through it. Tailor long-term-plan work activities with this in mind. Some ideas: alphabetize or color-sort the bookshelf, organize the toothbrush drawer, fold a basket of laundry, flatten the boxes for recycling, etc.
- Set up an agenda for the day. Post it on the fridge. Think of Marissa's time-blocking success. After basic responsibilities are taken care of (shower, make bed, etc.), give three options for a household helper activity, something that's kind of fun but also helpful. After the household helper activity, *then*

comes the list of fun activities: reading for pleasure, drawing, painting, lanyards, making a necklace, writing a letter, daydreaming on the hammock, practicing piano. Because the day requires the less-fun items to be completed earlier and leads up to free play, the free-play activities are much more enjoyable by comparison. Leisure activities become more enjoyable when they are part of the work-rest rhythm. Without work, leisure becomes dull in itself, and kids will simply crave more digital entertainment. With a daily agenda, your kids begin to understand how gratifying it can feel to be a contributing member of a household.

- If you have a hole in your work schedule, spend it reading or playing a game with your little one. The eye-to-eye contact will give them a boost that will last through independent playtime as you return to work tasks.

Remember *Bird Box* parents ("All tech bad. No screens ever.")? We are not them. I have advised several working parents who have those once or twice per week times that they MUST have quiet and simply cannot be interrupted in their work: Do not stress out if your long-term plan includes the occasional movie or specific and approved TV show for your children. If your kids experience one or two high-quality movies or shows per week, you will not derail your detox results. In fact, this can even be a wonderful bonding opportunity for siblings.

For older kids, you may have decided that you want to limit their video gaming to an hour per week. For a working parent, it might make the most sense to allow that window during the week while you are working, instead of on the weekend. That said, I would recommend a movie over video games for the reasons explained in chapter 9.

Either way, we are talking about discrete, defined technology, not a free pass to sit on YouTube unsupervised or play unlimited video games.

As the parent, you are the person best positioned to observe what amount of digital entertainment is feasible for your child without undermining your detox results and long-term plan. Studies show that a teenager's risk of depression and suicide begins to increase after two hours per day spent on new media (smartphones, games, social media). Risk factors skyrocket after five hours per day.[1] You can use the studies as a guide, but gauge your kids. You know when they are acting withdrawn, ornery, grumpy, or distracted. If you have a hunch that screen time is playing a role in that, confidently adjust or remove it.

Working parents will need to adjust when and how their long-term plan will best serve their families. But this is true of every type of family. Don't let shame and guilt lurk into the conversation. You are continually nudging your kids toward creating, inventing, exploring *while* erecting barriers and limits that best suit your family's needs. The process may not be easy, but you have what it takes to do the job. Assess and change as you need to. Expect friction, expect mistakes, but the time and energy you are investing in your kids is worth it.

What if I homeschool?

It can be very challenging to homeschool older children while keeping tiny ones from giving themselves a Sharpie facial, plucking the cat's whiskers, or setting the house ablaze (level of destruction depends on the child).

We underwent our family's detox while homeschooling older children, with two three-year-olds afoot. You can absolutely do this successfully—even if you are a homeschooling parent who previously relied on tech entertainment to keep your tiniest kids occupied. You will be pleasantly surprised to find that your smallest children thrive when they are not overstimulated by tablets and iPhone apps.

But how do you get your previously screen-entertained tinies hooked on new diversions while you attempt to teach big kids?

I'm going to tell you, ironically, through recounting a favorite TV series.

Remember the show *Lost*? It was all the rage in the early 2000s. The show included a smoke monster, and possibly a traveling island. I don't recall many details, but I definitely remember the cosmically important button. It had to be pressed every 108 minutes. If the button wasn't pressed, something awful would happen, like the world would explode, or Taco Bell would stop selling Mexican pizzas. The button would be pressed, and then the timer would start over, until 108 minutes later, when the button required another pressing.

Why are we talking about *Lost* and buttons? Because if you homeschool the big kids while removing all screen entertainment from your littles, you now have your own precious human buttons. Every so often, five to ten minutes initially, you will need to walk over and press the button. Your tiny kids will need you to get them started or nudged along on the screen-free activity that you have selected. If they have been accustomed to tablets or other overstimulating entertainment media, their time windows might start smaller. Younger kids also have smaller windows of time. The more they play without screens, the longer those time periods will stretch, because their attention spans and perseverance are growing. Familiarize yourself with when-ish their window of explosion will near, and check in before that. Observe how the window of time gets longer and longer as the weeks pass. Sure, you will have setbacks—sometimes your buttons will require pressing every four minutes. Or you might even miss a button press and a small meltdown will occur. But the long-term growth trend will be upward. So stay the course! (My attorney told me to make sure we all understand that "pressing your buttons" means "lovingly providing a new activity or encouragement for your child.")

Please do not mistake my suggesting that this can be done with great success for the false notion that it will be easy. Lord knows

I spent many a homeschool lunch break crying into my Lean Cuisine. But now, I can hand my four-year-old a puzzle or stack of books and he will play contentedly for forty-five minutes.

Homeschool mom Megan shared that one morning during her family's detox, she was babysitting another small child, in addition to her two toddlers. Megan had always allowed her younger kids to watch a show or play on tablets while she homeschooled. "Before our detox, I thought that would be the easiest way to keep them occupied while I teach," she said. During her detox, Megan turned off the shows and kept the iPads away. What happened? "No screens, and they played on their own the entire time—they only came around for snacks." It would have been worth the detox even if it was hard, but it wasn't! Don't you love those mom wins?

The pleasant surprise along the digital detox journey is that the friction and stress will become reduced as you do the difficult work up front. This is another valuable lesson for your kids. Soon they see that honing skills and delaying gratification pays off. Soon you will notice that your tiniest pupils will have an attentional readiness you weren't expecting. All because you did the hard but worthwhile thing. You go, Mom and Dad!

What if my family is on a budget?

Here is the beauty of screen-limited living: It is cheaper than dirt (which also happens to be a fine material for screen-free play). In fact, if you reapportion the money you previously spent on video games, tablets, etc., you will find more than enough available for supplies to help your kids create and enjoy the real world rather than electronics.

As you enter detox mode, you will likely find that your kids begin to rediscover the games, toys, and supplies already in your home. That was true for our family, and for many families who detoxed and reported back their results.

Here are some ideas for free and screen-free kid fun:

library books, art kits, and essay contests
couch forts
leaf art (collect leaves outside, glue to paper)
nature walk
drawing scenery
learning a skill from a library book
writing to a pen pal
playing in the sand
creating a fairy village out of rocks, sticks, dirt

When friends and family ask what types of gifts to buy for your kids' birthdays or holidays, request the kinds of supplies that will set your family up for success with your long-term plan. Which toys encourage kids to mindlessly consume tech? Which put children in the position to create and explore?

Don't accept every single one of your kids' desires and tendencies as immutable forces of nature. It may be "natural" for your child to want to paint the walls of your home with nail polish. But that doesn't mean we should allow or encourage that desire. By the same token, we shouldn't simply accept our kids' tendency to binge video games or TikTok scrolling. There is another way. Dr. Leonard Sax urges parents to "educate desire" in their children. Cultivate the good, steer away from the less desirable. It's our job.

When your kids dream up their birthday list requests, when Grandma asks what they hope to receive, help them! They might think they would like the newest Grand Theft Auto game, but by gently reminding them, "You will not play that game in our house before hell freezeth over," you can then pivot to other, different ideas. Birthdays and Christmas are great opportunities to think ahead: What gifts will continue to serve your child well throughout the year? Some inexpensive ideas:

reams of paper

art supplies

LEGO

blocks

glue

paint from the dollar store

Our Instagram feeds make us feel like every child wakes up in coordinated pajamas and can afford monthly craft box subscriptions. But an Instagram feed is not a realistic sampling of normal peoples' everyday-ness. It's a highlight zone. And highlight zones are fantastic, so long as we remember that is what they are. Instagram can also be a helpful place to follow like-minded parents on a budget who share great ideas for inexpensive screen-free diversions. There are plenty.

Remember, for most of history, kids have not had access to any addictive screen diversions. Create a culture in your home that shows your kids they don't have to keep up with the Kardashians. Almost half of the world's population lives on less than $5.50 per day. Take a breath, stay in reality, and get back to basics. Here's what your kids need from you: attention, love, limits, and conversation.

What about during emergencies like, I don't know, a worldwide pandemic, for example?

When the COVID-19 lockdown shuttered schools and kept all families at home, my family really enjoyed being home together. My husband's job was stable, and he simply worked out of our garage. Our kids' school moved online, so I was able to see them more often throughout the day. Once the IT kinks were figured out, we kind of loved being around each other. This is not to say there wasn't friction. Oh, heavens, do not misunderstand. Sibling fighting was still a thing, but so was bonding, football on the lawn during lunchtime, unrushed mornings, and less pressure to finish the laundry because, well, sweatpants.

I read article after article explaining that screen time SOARED over the course of the pandemic year, that parents' fears about losing their kids to the digital realm skyrocketed, that parents threw screen limits out the window. I was grateful that these numbers didn't apply to us. But the fact of the matter was simply this: Our detox and creation of a long-term plan a year *before* lockdowns prepared us *for* the lockdown. Of course, this was not because of my amazing planning skills. The timing happened to work out this way.

We found a path through the electronic entertainment quicksand. It's not because we are special or have a superpower. We are a normal family who simply unplugged it all, and then made an intentional plan for screen use in the home. We use tech as a tool to create, we use it to connect with each other. When it comes to consuming digital entertainment alone, we do that infrequently. Our littlest kids do it never. That's it. That is the secret. Anybody can do it.

A CNN reporter reached out to me several months into COVID-19 shutdowns. She was doing a story about the alarming rise in screen time, how parents felt they had no other options during a pandemic.

"Many families have thrown tech limits out the window right now," she said. "I know you did a digital detox on your kids awhile back. . . . But now, because of the current situation, has your family thrown out your screen limits? Have your kids been using more?"

"If you don't count school, no," I told her. "The kids are required to attend school on Zoom, which is not ideal because kids learn best in person. But in terms of fun and leisure? No. We have always enjoyed family movies together once or twice a week. That's basically it. When we detoxed our kids, we took that time to intentionally create a sustainable plan that works for our family.

We've tweaked it over time as the kids get older. But thankfully, the plan has worked, even in a pandemic!"

"Really?" she asked. It sounded like my response was different from the other folks she was interviewing for her piece on soaring screen time. "That's so great. I really appreciate your time."

Unsurprisingly, she did not include me in her story.

I hesitated sharing that with you because it could come across as slightly obnoxious, and I don't mean to pat myself on the back. Instead, I hope the takeaway is that this is doable for *anyone*! Parents should know that there is another way through family emergencies, and even worldwide emergencies. When everything hits the fan, we don't have to turn to our devices. In fact, we've seen what happens when we do, and it's not good. Living life in the real world is the best way to plan for real-world emergencies. Teach your kids to turn to their parents, and to each other, in good times and in bad. This is the best way to help them navigate life now and in the future.

Single-parent households

No doubt, raising kids as a single parent is challenging on many levels. If you decide to change the status quo of screen use in your home, this new endeavor will certainly be more difficult, at least in the short-term.

Nevertheless, I believe you were divinely appointed to parent the child in your home. If you feel like your child can benefit from a screen reset, don't let the difficulty deter you. Yes, your detox requires a little more work on the front end. Once you find your groove, and after you have your long-term plan in place, you will often be able to hand your kids a stack of books with the same success rate as handing them an iPad.

I'm not promising perfection. What I am promising is that removing screen entertainment from your kids will provide a window into their hearts and minds, without the screen daze. Your conversations will not be cut short by the allure of an awaiting video game. Instead of having a sliver of their attention, you will have all of it. This is particularly beneficial for single parents who feel like there is never enough time with their kids, due to work and other household responsibilities. You bond much more with your kids in a fifteen-minute meal without digital interruptions than in thirty minutes of multitasked "time together." You will begin to more clearly see the parts of them that need work, the parts that need love, what makes them tick. Your time spent intentionally loving your kids is always worth it, and your digital detox and subsequent long-term plan is no exception.

Foster families with kids from trauma backgrounds

This is my favorite category of family to discuss when it comes to digital detoxes. Why? Because the results from digitally detoxed foster kids have been the most dramatic. Let me give you some examples:

Foster parents Pete and Shannon took placement of a three-year-old boy whose previous foster home reported that the boy's behavior was too difficult to manage. They could no longer keep him. The child's behaviors qualified him for emergency behavioral therapy. The boy initially was unable to walk a quarter of a mile on a flat path. Eighteen-month-old family members were lapping this little guy, who lacked stamina and muscle. He had clearly not played outside much. He talked a lot about watching TV previously. Pete and Shannon observed a zero-screens policy. Instead, the family colored pictures together, encouraged outdoor play, and took long walks. After only a few weeks, his behavioral and physical improvement could not have been starker. Therapists and social workers assessed this child after a few months in Pete and Shannon's home, and they determined that he no longer qualified for the intensive behavioral therapy. Certainly, there were many factors at play, but the boy's foster parents say that they have experienced the same results with other foster children: a night-and-day difference when kids are given a loving home without the powerful effect of excessive digital entertainment.

Foster and adoptive parents Chris and Brianna have four elementary-aged children. They digitally detoxed their kids after observing inattentiveness, disobedience, and WWE-style sibling fights. How did their detox go? After two weeks they reported, "Attitudes are down to almost nothing, fighting is at an all-time low, no complaints about being bored, all my kids are reading more without me asking, they are finding things to do during transitions rather than running around the house like chickens with their heads cut off." This family experienced a dramatic shift after two weeks. So dramatic, in fact, that they extended their detox. "We were going to try two weeks and here we are. . . . A month later, we are both still in disbelief of how different our children are. . . . We've never had better times as a family so consistently."

As foster parents ourselves, my husband and I have noticed similarly dramatic results while maintaining a screen-limited environment with teenagers from difficult backgrounds.

One unprompted comment we got from a fourteen-year-old foster daughter: "Do you guys not like screens, or what?"

"We actually love technology," I replied. "We find that using it sparingly makes everyone happier. Kind of unusual, I know. But it works!"

Ten days later, the same foster daughter admitted, "You know what? I actually feel really good when I'm not staring at a screen. When I'm spending time outside and reading more, I feel better."

A fifteen-year-old foster daughter stayed at our home for only one night. We asked her about her life, went for a walk, ate peanut butter sandwiches. The most basic possible stuff. She reached out to me a few days later. "I don't know why, but I didn't want to leave. Usually I stay in my room on my phone. The fact that I was out in the kitchen with you guys the whole time . . . it even surprised me!" Her phone had died within a few minutes of her walking through our door. My husband was about to offer her a charger so she could call a "friend," but I shot him daggers and handed her our landline instead. I knew that missing power cord was the reason she was in our kitchen eating and connecting, rather than in her room on her phone. The difference she noticed in herself and her response to person-to-person connection reminded me that unplugging over PB&J has become detrimentally uncommon. The fix is so, so simple.

Multigenerational homes

"My parents live with us, and they help often with our kids. I want to keep the positive results of our detox, but feel badly telling them they can't let our kids use an iPad when we aren't home."

This can be a delicate situation, but I have found that grandparents can sometimes be stronger advocates of less tech entertainment for kids than millennial parents. After all, older parents and grandparents managed to raise their kids without the sorts of screen inundation we have today. Ask them about it. What were their favorite parenting hacks when they were younger?

If they don't seem to have any qualms about letting young kids binge on screens, start friendly conversations about what you've been learning and reading. Tell them about the negative impacts of digital entertainment. Share a stat or fact at dinner. For example, "Today I read two really fascinating facts. Did you know that before small kids can learn to read, they need to have approximately one thousand books read aloud to them? I also read that too much screen time can cause developmental delays in young children."

By letting grandparents know how and why you're deciding to upend the status quo in your home, you are more likely to get their support. As you begin to determine your long-term plan, you will have already started to find tools to help your kids stay occupied and interested in nonscreen activities. As your parents observe the positive changes in your kids, they will be more motivated to support your efforts. And even when they aren't, your kids are growing in their ability to play independently and rely less on tech entertainment. Ask Grandma and Grandpa to share their favorite stories or games from childhood with your kids.

That said, if Grandma and Grandpa are graciously babysitting for you and would prefer to watch a great movie with their grandkids, this will not derail your detox or long-term plan. You can easily work in weekly movie with Grandma to your family's long-term plan.

Only-child households

"My son doesn't have siblings around to play with. I don't want him on screens all the time, but I feel like I'm depriving him when I limit screens, because he doesn't have other kids to play with."

Each type of household has its own unique challenges. While only children don't have playmates, parents of multiple-sibling homes struggle to navigate disputes between their kids. No situation is always ideal, all the time. More might be required of parents on occasion in order to get their only children started on a task, a game, an adventure. When parents spend a few minutes up front getting a child started with a puzzle, LEGO, blocks, a fort, a book—anything, really—a kid is much more likely to take off running than if you plop him down and leave. If your child can't do this yet, keep trying new activities.

Reach out to a neighbor or friend with a similarly aged child. Set up recurring playdates. In between playdates, have your child brainstorm ideas for the next one. Write letters or draw pictures to mail to friends. Consider getting a pet. Start a garden. Take up a long-term hobby like painting a giant canvas or building a birdhouse. Where there's a will, there's a way. And along the way, you are teaching your child to use what he has to make his own fun and solve problems. Developing these skills will help equip him for his education, career, and social life.

In sickness

When kids are stuck home from school with a virus, we have chosen to allow movies or quality shows. Don't stress out if your kid is laid out, sleeping, sniffling, and watching some Mom- or Dad-approved flicks. I can hardly think of a better way to use a sick day. (Although let this portion of your plan remain an unspoken understanding between you and your spouse, rather than a "Sick days mean movies!" type policy. An announcement of this sort has been known to create miniature Ferris Buellers.)

Kids with special needs

Mom Tina shared that her four-year-old son has a fine motor delay and sensory processing disorder. Tina is a busy mom of three who spends a lot of time working to help her kids through various therapies, including occupational and speech therapy. She also has a full-time job. Tina and her husband have spent a lot of time trying to address their son's inability to hold a pencil and draw on paper. Four days into their detox, Tina emailed me: "My son drew his first stick figure! This is huge! He has never drawn anything before. And he literally took the paper out himself, sharpened a regular pencil (we have big pencils, short ones, fat ones, smelly ones, colored ones, gadgets to help him hold one, and even a vibrating one) . . . and he drew it! I was so surprised and proud of him!"

Tina and her husband were thrilled at their son's milestone. She also shared bumps along their family's digital detox journey, including some grumpiness and complaints from kids. Much of this is an inevitable part of parenting three small kids. But the flecks of gold, the developmental milestones, and the mood improvements throughout this family's detox have been exciting and worth celebrating.

Parents of children with special needs are often finding that the technologies they thought were helping can actually hinder their kids' growth and development. These technologies are incredibly new, and parents are wise to ask questions.

Child psychiatrist Dr. Victoria Dunckley, in her book *Reset Your Child's Brain*, suggests that what she calls Electronic Screen Syndrome "takes the brain hostage and presents as the spitting image of a specific mental disorder."[2] Dunckley explains through studies and individual cases that several patients have been diagnosed with various conditions, but upon closer scrutiny their symptoms either resolved or drastically improved after following her own prescribed screen reset. She says that screen time can disguise itself or exacerbate several conditions, including obsessive compulsive disorder, anxiety, separation anxiety, panic attacks, trauma and attachment disorder, night terrors, tics, Tourette's syndrome, stuttering, autism spectrum disorder, and headaches. If your child has been diagnosed with any of these conditions, I highly recommend reading Dunckley's book, particularly chapter 3, "Insidious Shape-Shifter: How ESS Mimics a Wide Variety of Psychiatric, Neurological and Behavioral Disorders." (Of course, many neurological disorders have nothing to do with screens! But it's worth asking questions.)

Bottom line

Conducting a successful detox and implementing a long-term plan is life-giving for every type of family. I have witnessed this in my own home and through the testimonies of parents who have navigated their own detoxes. No matter what kind of family you have, if you desire to find a way for your kids to enjoy technology without getting sucked in, it can absolutely be done, and you are the person best suited for the task. Remember: A friction-free life is not a thing for anybody, no matter what your Instagram feed looks like. Every family has its own unique challenges to overcome. Putting technology in its proper place in your home—no matter what your home looks like—is a worthwhile endeavor, and an investment in your child's heart and mind.

12

Tech for Mom and Dad

We are forever elsewhere.

SHERRY TURKLE, *RECLAIMING CONVERSATION*

I WAS AN EXCESSIVELY CHATTY CHILD (she said, after talking for 199 pages now). Despite my incessant blabbing, Dad always listened. Even more remarkably, he always seemed interested. We spent many trips in the car together, driving around town. Dad loved listening to Steely Dan and the Beatles. Within a minute of cuing up his cassette tape, I would inevitably begin to share a story or observation. No matter how boring, Dad always turned down the volume. Always. Of my zillions of utterances from the passenger seat, I remember exactly none of what I shared with him. What remains in my mind is the sound of him turning down a song he loved in favor of listening to a seven-year-old butcher a joke she read on a Popsicle stick.

To a child, parental love is indistinguishable from parental attention. They are one and the same. Yet today's parents are giving kids a fraction of the attention we were given. While parents do spend more time *physically* caring for their kids than ever before, they are also more distracted than ever.

Sixty-five percent of mobile phone users report being ignored by somebody in their own house who chose the mobile device over the human. This number has increased over the past six years, breaking each previous year's record.[1]

This happens more than we care to admit. Too often parents fool themselves into thinking that physical proximity compensates for attentional unavailability. It doesn't. In order to create an emotional connection during the course of a conversation, the participants need to make eye contact 60 to 70 percent of the time. But today, adults make eye contact about half that amount.[2] Even our littlest kids know the difference. Half of parents report that their own kids have asked them to put their phones away.[3] Yikes.

Tech expert Linda Stone calls this "continuous partial attention."[4] The new status quo of splintered parental attention has robbed families of the love and warmth that has nurtured children's growing brains for millennia. The Nielsen company reports that the average American adult spends nearly eleven hours per day on some type of screen.[5] Between sleep, work, and driving, there's no way around it—a bulk of the time parents spend with their kids is "continuously partial."

Even though 79 percent of parents believe that they could improve their relationships with their kids if they all took a screen break,[6] "only 12 percent of adults say they intentionally set aside a time of day when they don't use electronics."[7]

More alarmingly, parents spend nearly the same amount of one-on-one time with their devices as they do with their kids, at two-plus hours per day.[8]

One report predicted that early millennials will experience one-third fewer face-to-face interactions with other people because of our cultural shift toward digitized lives.[9] This report came out in 2000. Can you imagine what the data might say for today's kids, after the invention of the iPhone and tablets?

We know what kids need from their parents. Too often, they aren't getting it.

I asked pediatric speech therapist Monica Gomez how she sees screen time impacting parenting. Her eyes got wide. "It's huge," she said. "When I urge parents to sit on the ground and play with their small kids, they stare at me blankly. They say, 'Like how? My child loves the iPad. Can you recommend an app instead?'"[10] This, even while the evidence is clear: Real-life parental attention and response is the most important nutrient for a child's brain. This speech therapist works with parents who are developmentally disabled. Initially, she was concerned that the children—who were developmentally normal—would have a difficult time catching up to peers because of their parents' disabilities. The opposite turned out to be true. "I couldn't believe it," she said. "The delayed parents understood better how to get on the floor and play with their kids. They didn't overcomplicate it, they just did it. And it made all the difference. Play, back-and-forth connection, and conversation with attentive parents—this is how kids grow and learn."

We know this is true intuitively, and the studies continue to prove it—loving parents, conversation, boundaries, attention. These are the primary ingredients for nurturing our children. Nevertheless, the family is being lured away from this fundamental truth by a mirage of empty digital promises. Despite knowing better, we pursue more distraction disguised as connection.

Unsurprisingly, kids are more depressed, more anxious, and lonelier than ever before.

We parents might need a course correction too.

Our attention is a finite resource

Parents have not set out to intentionally ignore their kids. It just . . . happens. In the daily grind, in the stress and chaos, sometimes it's easier to escape and scroll than to string plastic beads on a necklace, mediate a ridiculous LEGO spat, or listen to a long and inaccurate retelling of *Home Alone*. ("Sweetie, the main character's name is Kevin, not Home Alone. . . . No, you don't have to start the story over.")

What parent among us doesn't long for a tiny shot of dopamine, a little escapist Houzz hunting? I've never crushed candy personally, but can we really blame a bus-stop-waiting mom or dad who finally has all the octopus-children restrained in car seats? Sometimes parents just need a break, man.

It's in this quest for relief and escape that parents scroll. And it's entirely relatable. We've all been there. The problem is the unseen opportunity costs.

We had our first three kids in three years. That season was not easy. Some days, it was all I could do to crawl across the finish line in the same pajamas I woke up in that morning. My husband would reassure me, "It will not be like this forever. They will not be in diapers forever. They won't always scream irrationally when you buckle them into their car seats." Frankly, I didn't believe him. Because I was in the midst of it. I couldn't see past the hard. But he was right. Looking back, I wish that I had numbered those days instead of rolling my eyes at people who told me to enjoy them.

Today, as I parent six kids, I am more mindful of the speed at which they progress from one stage to the next. The longer we do this thing, the more disciplined I've become at pressing into the hard parts instead of wishing them away. It hasn't gotten easier, but I've gotten better at it. Functionally, it feels easier.

The fact of the matter is that we parents are already serving our guts out for our kids. We wake up all night with the babies. We get them dressed into their third outfit by eleven a.m. (Thank you, potty training.) We work so hard to help them start walking and talking, until they do. And then we train them to sit down and be quiet. We wash their insanely dirty clothes and answer zillions of questions. We wipe snot from tiny nostrils. We put them to bed, only to do it all over again. We are exhausted, and understandably so. We are laboring our faces off. But what we miss too often is the most critical part, the best part.

It happens every day. We come to the end of ourselves in service to our kids. We have met every external need, and we finally see a tiny glimpse of quiet and rest. It's so close, we can taste it: The dino nuggets are served, kids are happy and quiet. We have a choice in that moment: escape and scroll OR give it one last push—pull up our own chair. Sit down, look in their eyes, and get into their hearts, with 100 percent of our attention.

"If you could go anywhere in the world, where would it be?"

"What's something that makes you laugh?"

"If you had a zillion dollars, what would you do with it?"

"Is there anything that makes you feel scared?"

Families are being robbed of these conversations by electronic diversions. If it's not our kids' attention that's digitally hijacked, it's our own. We are missing out because we choose the easier thing instead of the worthwhile thing. We spend so much time and energy caring for the physical needs of our kids that the ground is fertile and ready for emotional and spiritual cultivation. Yet it's in that very moment we turn to our phones. The days are long, and we are exhausted. Sometimes the last thing we want to do is give that last 3 percent of our remaining energy to what feels like a pointless conversation. But this is exactly what our kids need. They need us to draw out their feelings and fears, to speak life into their hearts and dreams. They need our eye contact. They need us to pick up the book and read it aloud. To genuinely take interest in the Popsicle stick joke as they butcher it. The push-through, the using up of our last 3 percent of parental battery life, is hard. But that is where you find the best parental treasures.

Recently, I was making dinner at the end of a long day. I was exhausted. Several kids buzzed around the kitchen, making noise and asking random questions. I wanted to tune out, but instead I tuned in. I turned to my four-year-old foster son, who had been with our family for about a year. "Buddy, do you remember coming to our house for the first time?"

"Yes," he said.

"What did you think about that?"

"At first it was scary, and it was a stranger's house. But then it was just my mom and my dad."

This took my breath away. I'd never heard him say anything like it. In foster parenting, and regular parenting for that matter, many days feel like one obstacle after the next. But we don't always see what is happening under the surface, the unseen fruit of our parental labor. Unless we ask.

That little fleck of gold from my foster son will live in my heart forever. I replayed it in my mind and it got me through disciplinary struggles with a different child the next day. Because I knew that all the love, work, and intentional conversations we parents pour in are cultivating beautiful unseen tapestries of life and healing. And I never would have seen this glimpse if I had checked out instead of pouring in.

There's been a troubling trend in parenting over the last decade or so. In the name of authenticity and "keeping it real," we complain about the hard parts of parenting, air all of our shortcomings, and then congratulate each other. "I'm so glad I'm not the only one who yells at my kids/lets them watch five hours of YouTube. That's just the way I am!" It's an okay start, but we can't stop there. That would be like showing up to an AA meeting, saying, "I'm an alcoholic. Phew! Glad I got that off my chest," and then everyone high-fives and hits the bar. Wouldn't it be better if we used this refreshing new wave of real-life sharing to exhort and encourage each other to do better? Not in shame or blame, but in mutual striving to live out our calling well.

Protect your breaks instead of multitasking them

To be clear, parents need breaks. Breaks are not optional, and we must protect them. Show me a human who has put in too many consecutive parenting hours, and I will show you a clip of *Saved by the Bell*'s Jessie Spano on caffeine pills. Sadness, anger, hunger, twitching—you name it, overworked parents feel it.

We must create windows for breaks. For me, it means rising while it's dark to read in a quiet house. It also means regular date nights. And setting up a moms' night out with friends. For dads, that might look like poker nights, golfing, or hiking with friends. Find your chosen method of taking well-deserved breaks, and do not skip them, for the love of Zack Morris.

The important distinction between taking breaks and giving your kids your last 3 percent of battery life is this: Stop multitasking your parenting and your breaks. Stop trying to squeeze in a minute of Facebook scrolling as your kid plays next to you. It's confusing for your brain and for your kids, and it leads to frustration. It also makes your kids feel ignored, like they are less important than your phone. Instead, schedule some specific windows to veg out so you can leave the phone behind while your kids are around.

Who doesn't love multitasking in the name of productivity? But the research actually shows that we should think twice before doing it. In fact, 98 percent of the population cannot effectively divide attention between two tasks at the same time.[11] We are fooling ourselves to think we can parent well while scrolling. "Multitasking gives us a neurochemical high," so we start to feel pretty great about ourselves. What is actually happening? "Our performance degrades for each new task we add to the mix."[12] Multitasking has also shown to increase stress.

Instead of firing off an email during your walk with your child, block your time to finish your important tasks while she reads, makes bracelets, weaves baskets, etc. "Sweetie, after I'm done with this task, I'm all yours." Then take that walk, fully focused on your daughter. Notice how much more enjoyable your time together is.

In early motherhood with two kids under two, I exhaustedly told our pediatrician that I could hardly juggle every responsibility.

My fifteen-month-old was active and curious. She wanted my attention all day. But so did her baby brother, the laundry, the dishes. What could I do? Her response: "Spend ten to fifteen uninterrupted minutes with your one-year-old."

That's it? I thought. *Seriously? Spend time with my kid? This lady has no clue how hard my life is.* Then I tried it. And she was 100 percent right. When I fully focused on my daughter, I filled her tank, and she was able to play independently for longer stretches. I, in turn, had more opportunities to take much-needed breaks.

A decade and five kids later, I still use this trick. I recently read several picture books aloud to my three smallest kids. After fifteen or so minutes, I told them that it was time to read independently. I picked up my book. They each grabbed one from our library stack. And we quietly enjoyed our reads, by the hearth and by each other's side—for an hour. (I should mention, these kids were three, five, and five at the time. None were fluent readers. They can still enjoy picture books alone.) A full tank and the mentor approach leave space for both desired connections and much-needed breaks.

Moving forward

When you decide to get fit, you start by stepping on the scale. You need to check your baseline so you know how far you need to go before reaching your goals. Austrian management consultant Peter Drucker said, "That which gets measured gets managed." This is why we are taking a closer look at our own tech use. Maybe you'll measure it, inspect it, and think, *Hey, I'm doing all right. My kids say they don't feel ignored or less important than my phone. I don't feel stressed or unproductive, and the time my screen says I spend on it is the same as the amount I planned to spend on it.* If so, great!

You might check your screen use and think, *Hmm. This says I spent three hours on my phone yesterday. One of those hours was spent video chatting with Callie's therapist, and the other was banking and grocery shopping. Looks like I don't have much fat to trim.* Great!

Or you could look at your phone use and think, *Six hours yesterday?! I don't feel like I spend this much time on social media, because it's a little bit here and there, but my screen time app shows me that it adds up. I enjoy social media, but I don't want this proportion of my waking hours to be spent on it.*

Wherever you land, it's wise for us to check our metrics and compare them to where we want to be. It's also important that our kids see us acknowledging our own vulnerabilities and then taking action.

As you and your spouse take inventory of your own technology use, I'd like to recommend a helpful marriage principle we learned at our church: "Draw a circle around yourself and fix everyone within the circle." Essentially, it is your job to check and reflect on your own use, and let your spouse check and reflect on his or her own tech use. If both parties are honestly and intentionally working to examine their own tech use and evaluate potential shortcomings, you will find growth in this arena, without a free ticket to the spousal blame-game rodeo. Yee-haw.

One warning: If you don't think anything inside your circle needs help, you may want to use a mirror or phone a friend. Humbly ask your spouse or kids, "Do you ever feel ignored because I'm using my phone (or iPad, game, computer, Netflix)? Any other ways you think my tech use gets in the way of our real-life connection?" I know, it's uncomfortable to invite criticism, but if you have honestly taken inventory and found nothing wrong, you might benefit from the input of somebody close to you. They might agree with your assessment. Or they might not. One last tip for this conversation: Respond with, "Thank you for sharing that with me. I'd like to take some time to think about that." And then do that.

Making the best use of tech for Mom and Dad

It's helpful to approach conversations about digital media use not in terms of right and wrong, but in terms of "in its right place." Because, of course, digital media can be incredibly useful and fun, and even facilitate the connection all humans need.

Sometimes when I encourage parents to limit tech, there is push-back. I completely understand this, because for years, I was the parent who pushed back. Sometimes parents will say, "Wasn't the response to the printing press similarly alarmist? Didn't people worry that people would check out of real life because their faces would be stuck in books?"

Yes, we could make any technology, any *thing*, a master, an idol. But we are talking about tech overuse because the research is showing that's today's threat. Our sanity, our relationships with our kids, our ability to enjoy life are being hampered. "Screen Time 'reduces talk time between parent and child by 85% when the screen is on,'" according to Dr. Ari Brown of the American Academy of Pediatrics.[13] Studies, research, and the settings on our own phones are revealing to us the places where the bulk of our attention is going.

We are a special generation of parents. I know, it's such a millennial thing to declare. But it's true. The current generation of parents holds a unique perspective. We have one eye on our own childhoods: dirt, neighbors, treehouses, bikes, awkward group dates to the mall. And we have one eye on our kids': social media, iPad obsession, weak, bored, grumpy. *We* are best equipped to show them the way. We must rise to the occasion, and we must start with ourselves.

Putting parental tech in its proper place

"The most vibrant, healthful relationship with tech begins with none."[14]

So I detoxed myself. I also recruited several parents who detoxed their kids alongside me, because everything is better in community. In setting up our parental detox plans, we soon realized that we couldn't exactly go cold turkey, because phones are how parents communicate with teachers, doctors, dentists, social workers, and family. I also grocery shop, bank, and write on my phone. I check in with friends—and even help coach other parents through their kids' detoxes—over text or Voxer. Perhaps it's true that the best relationship with tech begins with none. But unless we decided to start life over in an underground bunker, screen detoxing adults was proving to be much more complicated.

One detoxing parent, Tina, works full-time in the medical field. She spends ten-hour days charting on her computer. Another helps care for an ailing parent, including bills and facilitating medical care. Everyone has a unique life situation. So we created individually tailored plans to put tech in its proper place. That meant more of a screen reduction than a full-blown cold-turkey detox. We each created detox plans that worked for our unique lives.

For two weeks, here is what my plan looked like for me:

- I will keep my phone off my person. My phone will sit in its charging dock, not my pocket.
- I will delete all social media apps. Because I share my writing on these platforms, I allowed myself to use them via computer, twice a day for ten minutes or less, so that I could post my writing and reply to messages.
- I deleted my email app. Instead, I created specific windows for checking email at my computer: ten minutes in the morning, ten minutes at lunch.
- I took a break from podcasts.
- Work-related tech use was, of course, allowed.

I did this for two weeks. Here's how it went:

- Phone use decreased 60–80 percent over the course of two weeks. This shocked me. I didn't think I had been using social media or email as often as I was. But the metrics don't lie. The craziest thing? I didn't feel deprived of social media—I didn't even miss it. The only thing I removed was habitual, mindless scrolling. I kept the best parts: deliberate connection.

- One day, I had plopped my little girls into the bathtub and sat on a nearby stool to supervise. I reached for my phone before realizing that there was nothing fun on it to do. So I turned back to my bathing beauties. I chatted with them, enjoying their sweet giggles and splashes. My attention toward my kids shifted from partial to deep, from mechanical to enjoyable.

- Deleting my most-used apps attentionally demagnetized my phone. At times I would glance toward it, but now it looked different. Boring, even. Other parents who detoxed shared similar findings.

- Another morning, while the kids were eating breakfast, I picked up my coffee and turned toward my phone. I would typically open Instagram at this point. But it wasn't there. So instead, I sat at the table with my kids, sipping my coffee and asking them about their most recent art projects. This happened a handful of times during the two-week period. Mom Caitlin shared that during her detox, she took her kids to the park. Instead of using that time to scroll through Instagram, she watched her kids. "I realized the other day that my twelve-year-old son is on his last days of saying, 'Mom, watch this!' Someday soon, he will never say that again."

- I read more books. I read a lot anyway, but I noticed that when my kids ask me for something while I'm scrolling my phone, sometimes my knee-jerk reaction is annoyance, which isn't good. But when they talk to me while I'm reading a book, it doesn't feel like an interruption. My mind has an easier time shifting my attention from a book to my kids.

- My life pace felt different. The pre-detox status quo would pull me out of real life for a few minutes, long enough to feel flustered and behind when I put my phone down. Then my internal pacing was stressed and out of sync. During my detox, my pace synced up with my kids' pace.

- Pre-detox, when I was listening to a podcast and my kids simply asked me a question, I would sometimes respond impatiently while I paused it. I am concerned that my kids get the sense that they are interrupting me when they are simply trying to talk to me. My detox window allowed me the space to notice this. I want my kids to feel like the default is that they can come talk to me anytime, and they will be met with warmth and love. If an external trigger shifts my response into annoyance toward my kids, I need to reevaluate that. Podcasts can be informative and life-giving to me. But as I work them back into regular life, I am more aware of my own vulnerabilities.

- I realized that I had frequently been picking up my phone out of habit rather than interest.

Hiccup-type moments:

- I was running errands, which included a quick trip to the grocery store to buy snacks for my kindergartners' class. There were very specific snacks the teacher had requested due to allergy concerns. I could not remember which snacks. I would have checked my email, but I had deleted my app, and the slow internet in the store wasn't cooperating. I had to call my husband at work to look it up on my email. That was kind of inconvenient.

- I felt so free when I didn't care about my phone. "Where's my phone? I don't know, and I don't care!" Like Mary Tyler Moore joyously throwing her hat into the air. Except that other people did care. I missed important phone calls from my husband and others more than once. This left me longing for some kind of technology halfway between smartphones and the home phone days of yore.

- At one point I totally broke my own detox rules. But I had to! There was some drama unfolding in a local Facebook parenting group. I heard through the grapevine that there was misinformation being spread about a dear friend. My inner detective had to investigate. Thirty minutes later, I am embarrassed to report, my time was not at all well spent. I closed my computer feeling anxious and annoyed. (DUH.)

Creating a feasible long-term plan for parents

There were several components of my detox that I kept long-term.

1. **Remove notifications from all apps.** Why did we ever allow notifications in the first place? I would never give a stranger or an acquaintance permission to enter my home, walk up, and tap me on the shoulder. Yet this is what we do when we allow apps to pull our attention away from real life. Removing notifications converts your phone to a place more like your physical mailbox. Would you let the pizza coupon flyer man walk into your home and hand you a $2-off coupon in the shower? Not unless he wants a jujitsu demonstration on his face. A few moments later, a high school acquaintance knocks on your bathroom door to hand you a picture of her lunch. No. These people can put all their messages in one place, and we don't need to be alerted when they arrive. *We* decide when we will check it. *We* decide when and where to allocate our attention. Thank you, and good day, sirs.

2. **Create windows to intentionally check on your digital life.** I have yet to meet a parent who has decided they want to be on their phone all day. For most parents, it just happens. This is why it helps to declare specific windows for enjoying your apps. Pick your times and stick to it. You want to check your stock portfolio, personal email, social media, hilarious meme pages, and news every day. Great. Create spaces for that. Decide what is feasible for you: for twenty minutes before the kids wake up, at lunch for five minutes—whatever makes sense for your life. When you feel the inner nudge to wander into digital spaces outside of the windows you have created, simply tell yourself, "No, it's not time for that right now." If you can't stick to the plan you have decided you want, then that means one of two things: (1) maybe you've set an unrealistic plan, or (2) maybe your plan *is* realistic and reasonable, but you need to erect some barriers or get some accountability to help you stick to it. If you want an additional barrier, you could even set parental controls on your phone and give the password to your spouse or friend.

3. **There will be mistakes, but use them to do better.** We aren't expecting perfection from our kids or from ourselves. But we are expecting growth in an area that we have decided to work on. If you are missing the mark, don't beat yourself up. Troubleshoot. Share around the dinner table with your kids that you are still figuring this out too. Share technologies that you find incredibly useful or fun. Share the ones that you find addictive. You are a human being responding to technology that was designed to keep you hooked. You are not unusually weak or flawed when your brain responds to a stimulus that was engineered to stimulate it. The way we mentor our kids through our own tech-life balance is just as important as our rules for them.

A final takeaway

If we aren't careful, we will turn away from our flesh and blood, carelessly giving away our most precious asset: our attention. Worse, we will give it away to inanimate objects, leaving our wide-eyed beauties waiting quietly and growing quickly. They deeply desire to be influenced and cultivated by Mom and Dad. With some humility and simple planning, we can put tech in its right place. Then we don't have to feel guilty about using it, because we have already vetted it and sorted it. Now we can enjoy it, the way *we* intend to (purposeful, defined), not the way *it* wants us to (aimless, constant, automatic). When we do, we find a similar life-hack that we gifted our kids. We no longer feel tethered, stuck, or rushed.

Our kids are watching us. They are experiencing the full range of human feelings, fears, curiosities, and pleasures—just like us, only in smaller clothes. They are learning how to process their anxieties and desires by watching us. We are their coaches, their fans, their authorities, their teachers, and most importantly, their moms and dads. They have so much to learn and share. We have the privilege of drawing their hearts' burdens out from the inside and into words. We get to look into their beautiful faces and speak life to them along the way. The stakes are so high. But we can rise to the occasion.

What's that? You haven't done it perfectly? Welcome to the club, my friend. Literally everyone is in it. Maybe we haven't done it perfectly so far, but we need not stress. Remember those brain scientists who told us that we can rewire our kids' brains to be happier and healthier, based on the experiences we give them? Well, the ability to rewire brains isn't exclusive to children and teens. It is true for all of us, young and old.[15]

I hope you finish this book confident that you have everything you need to parent your kids well in a world drowning in entertainment disguised as progress. You get to steer them through the mess. You are the person called to teach them how to enjoy but not obsess, taste but not binge.

For too many kids today, digital life doesn't *impact* their world, digital life *is* their world. But it doesn't have to be that way. Parents have the privilege of introducing our kids to a different way. A way that prizes real-life, person-to-person connection, conversation, and love. A way that uses technology as a tool to improve our lives, not waste them. You have been divinely appointed to guide your children through this exact point in time. You can do it.

Afterword

MY DAD WORKED in the entertainment industry for decades, writing and producing TV shows. What some might call "mindless television" put food on our table and sent me to college. I enjoyed television and video games as a child, and I still do. If you're looking for someone to decry all technology, you've come to the wrong place. I don't just love technology, I love digital entertainment. I approach it in the same way I approach chocolate donuts: in moderation.

My childhood was marked by warmth and connection, even while I enjoyed digital entertainment. But the temptation to wholly displace parental influence in the '80s and '90s was nothing like it is today. The collective substitution of parental connection with endless digital entertainment has come upon us in the same way Ernest Hemingway described bankruptcy in *The Sun Also Rises*: "gradually, then suddenly." Some could argue we're teetering on a collective attentional and relational bankruptcy.

But I'm hopeful for the future, because I've seen the overnight and lasting change in my kids, and in dozens of other kids whose parents included me in their journeys.

Three years after our detox, I'm blown away by the growth in my kids. I asked my eleven- and twelve-year-old kids, "What have you noticed since our detox three years ago?"

My son said, "I get along better with my brothers and sisters. We fight less. I feel less grumpy. And it's easier to pay attention in school."

My daughter said, "I used to read sometimes, but I would rather play Minecraft. Now I still like Minecraft, but I'd only want to play it like once a week. . . . I didn't realize that playing outside is so much more fun."

As much as I wish we could put our kids in a parenting machine and pop out perfection a few years down the road, that is not a thing. Kids are unique humans with personalities and proclivities all over the map. But most parents I talk with (me included) want to be faithful to our calling. We want to shepherd our kids well with the tools that we have. To that end, I hope this book has helped serve as a guide to paddle through the rough waters. If not, it can at least double as a swatting mechanism to gently keep unruly wildlings from approaching the iPad. (I kid.)

This parenting gig ain't for the faint of heart. But for the valiant among us, we rise to each occasion of stress, setback, and cultural trend. We don't ignore trials because they're hard. We face them head-on. Cheers to you for rolling up your sleeves to invest in your child, despite living in a world telling you to leave them to their own devices.

I would love to hear how your family's detox went! You can find me at www.mollydefrank.com.

Tips for Getting a Skeptical Spouse on Board

REMEMBER: You and your spouse are on the same team.

You are making a loving appeal to your partner in life, the person you cultivate children with. You both want the best for your kids. You are simply hashing out tactics. Like business partners of a Fortune 50 company, you respect each other. You are proposing a transformative idea for your people.

- Your posture in this conversation is, "Hey, I have a great idea that might be our best parenting move yet."
- You are glowing with optimism and possibility.
- You are making the detox sound attractive. Imagine how much our kids can learn, grow, and accomplish with their newfound time!
- Smile.
- Bring a preliminary plan.
- Reassure your spouse that you aren't going all-out rogue Amish.

- Let your spouse know that you will want to bring back handpicked tech *after* your two-week detox. And you'll decide those details together.

Sample script

"Hey, babe. I was thinking I'd make [insert their favorite dinner] tonight. Sound good?

"Also, I've been thinking about the kids. About some of the tantrums/anger/disobedience/grumpiness/fighting/behavioral/attention issues we've been seeing. Have you noticed how it's worse after screen time? (Insert specific example or two.)

"I was researching more about it, and it turns out that their brains are being purposely triggered into fight-or-flight mode when they play some of these games. After a while, their brains begin to create so much dopamine that the dopamine receptors start to die. That's why kids say they're bored. They can't even sense enjoyment from normal life. There's a lot of neurological and psychological engineering that goes into the game designs. Anyway, there's this two-week digital detox plan I found. It's kind of like a fast, but for kids' digital entertainment. And it's only two weeks. Lots of parents have tried it and said the results blew them away. And it doesn't cost anything. The whole plan is in the book I already have.

"What if we tried it with our kids for two weeks? Then afterward, we'd decide how much and which types of tech we want to keep. I think it could be really good."

If your spouse is open to hearing more, share your preliminary plans:

"I already have a list of activities ready for when the kids say they're bored."

"We could start this Friday, because we will both be home and have all hands on deck."

"I've been talking to the neighbor/friend at church/family friend, and they're interested too. We can do it together, which will make it easier."

"We don't necessarily have to detox alongside the kids. Let's talk about it. What do you think?" (You can even concede to leave that part up to the unsure spouse!)

If your spouse says, "No way. That sounds too hard/crazy/ridiculous," leave them with, "Would you mind thinking about it? I'd really love to try this. I'm happy to take on more of the prep and planning since I'm more excited about it than you. Let's circle back and talk about it again tomorrow."

If your spouse has objections addressed in this book, ask if they'd be willing to read a few pages. Here are shortcuts to where I address common objections:

- "We grew up watching TV in the '80s and '90s. Isn't digital tech the same thing, but for the next generation?" See "Everything has changed" section of chapter 1, pages 28–30.
- "They need to be prepared for the future. Everything is online now. Even play." See "Myth busters" section of chapter 10, pages 173, 174.
- "All their apps and games are educational!" See "Myth busters" section chapter 10, pages 171–172.
- "This isn't feasible for us since we both work/my parents watch our kids/we homeschool." See chapter 11.

Some cautions:

- Do not introduce the idea in the middle of conflict, even if the conflict is related to screen time.
- Do not fold your arms.

- Do not come from a posture of "I am right, you are wrong."
- Do not use this conversation to point out what you dislike about your spouse's tech use habits.
- Do not enter the conversation with attitude, sass, or a chip on your shoulder.

Two-Week Detox Daily Plan

SOME PARENTS PREFER general guidance and principles as they implement their detox, which I've laid out throughout the book. (Remember, UNDO!)

For families who prefer more order and checklists and daily guidance, below you will find a sample of a daily format that might suit you.

This is a *sample* plan. Parenting is a lot more art than science. If you are following this daily plan and come across a task that does not appeal to your family, trade it out for an intentional connective option that does. Give yourself freedom to switch any task for one that better fits your people: ride quads on your property, jog together through Central Park, arrange flowers, stock the shelves at your family business. Make it your own.

Your daily tasks are simple:

1. Spend at least fifteen minutes of completely connective time with your child.
2. Observe your kids.
3. Stay the course.

As you're able, write your observations in your detox journal. Each day, note three things:

One hard thing

One victory

A quote from the children, good or bad

If you miss writing notes one day, or if your day three happens on day seven, that is FINE! The format below is meant to serve you, not the other way around.

Sample plan

Day 1

- ☐ Sit down with your kids and make your list of ideas for screen-free activities. Let them color, decorate, create supplemental artwork.
- ☐ Post your list near your calendar or in another visible place. Add illustrations for kids who can't yet read. A printable list of screen-free activity ideas is available at www.mollydefrank.com.
- ☐ Pay attention to your kids. Make mental notes of their strengths and weaknesses. Talk to your spouse and compare observations.

Day 2

- ☐ Visit the library. Bring the kids. Pick up the stack of quality books you've put on hold, and let your kids select and check out a few with their own library cards. Make it fun! (If this first trip is a disaster, take heart. It gets easier, and the kids are learning!) See chapter 5 for book suggestions and library outing tips.

Coaching tip: Imagine standing at the finish line of your detox—kids with longer attention spans and more patience, kids who can troubleshoot their own boredom, kids whose creativity drives them toward wonder and discovery. Make your parenting decisions today with that end goal in mind. Your short-term sacrifice is worth the long-term gain!

Day 3

☐ Grab one of your library books, a blanket, and any delicious snack. Head to the lawn, or even the living room if the weather isn't cooperating. Bring your best accents and read aloud. For older kids, read a chapter book. Take turns reading aloud to engage their attention. You are never too old for a good read-aloud.

Which toys, games, books, activities are your children gravitating toward? Note observations in your detox journal.

Day 4

☐ Take a short or long walk with your kids. Ask each to share a dream they hope to accomplish one day. Anything under the sun. Share one of your dreams with them.

In your journal, name an aspect of each child's character that is strong. Name an aspect that has a lot of potential for growth.

Day 5

☐ Teach your children to play checkers, chess, or a favorite card game. Play a round or two. Teach siblings to play with each other, and get them started while you take care of all the parenting things. (There will likely be friction.

That's okay! Teach your kids the rules and how to navigate losing and winning graciously.) For the only child, try a Rubik's cube or the game Perfection.

What nonscreen talents are you noticing in your children?

Day 6

☐ Grab a snack, dessert, or yummy beverage. Sit down with your children and ask them to teach you something they know that you don't. A few piano notes? How to dab? What is the coolest shoe right now? Ask your younger children to teach you a dance or how to draw a rainbow. Ask your older kids what keeps them awake at night. Listen well.

Check in with your spouse, babysitters, other caregivers. What are your observations so far?

Day 7

☐ You're halfway through! Great work. Check in with your kids. Ask them to share one thing they have liked about not having screen entertainment for a whole week.

Day 8

☐ Turn on your kind, sweet parent voice. Ask your children to help you with a task (something not already part of their chore responsibilities). Anything. Sort laundry. Empty the dishwasher. Do not match their annoyance or frustration. Instead, lovingly beckon them. "I know what you mean, sometimes chores feel unfun. But it's all how you view it. When I resent my chores, I try to replace my resentment with gratitude. Like, 'Thank you, God, for hands to empty this dishwasher. Thank you for running water to clean our dirty dishes. Thank you for blessing me with children who need to eat. Thank you that I don't have to wash these all by hand!'" As you work together, enjoy the silence, let your children share an observation or thought. Listen. Ask a question. Be patient. When the task is complete, you can offer to help them with one of their chores. You may also notice that your children make themselves scarce after the chore is done. Amazing how their ability to entertain themselves spikes when potential chores are the alternative.

Day 9

☐ Ask your children to tell you about a person they admire. What traits do they find admirable in that person? Tell your children about a person you admire. Tell them the traits you try to emulate in your heroes. Affirm your children's giftings and strengths. Together, think of ways to use those gifts today. Shoot hoops? Practice artwork? Play the drums? Shoot pool?

Coaching tip: Don't lose heart if your children are not celebrating their digital fast. You are absorbing your children's short-term frustration for their long-term well-being. This is not forever. Using your parental observational superpowers, look for ways to cultivate your children. Even in the tiny windows of drive time, meal prep, playing catch, there are seeds to be sown, and it's your job to sow them. You got this!

Day 10

☐ During dinner, read or tell the story of Cain and Abel, Jacob and Esau, or any other disastrous sibling pairing.

Talk about what it looks like for siblings to love and care for one another versus having envy, fighting, and tricking one another. Share some sibling stories from your youth. Ask what kind of relationship your kids hope to have with their siblings. What can they do today to help grow that kind of relationship?

Day 11

☐ Based on talents or interests you've observed in your children, take them somewhere to feed that interest. Skateboarding? Hit the skate park. Biking? Head to the local park with bike jumps. Gardening? Visit the nursery and look around. Animals? Head to the zoo or pet shop. Doesn't need to take up an entire day. Give your child as much of your full attention as possible.

Day 12

☐ Ask your children which types of books they want to place on hold at the library. Based on the selections they've leafed through or read, do they enjoy fantasy? Graphic novels? Joke books? Fact books? Picture books? Funny books? Do a little research in the genre they've identified and find those with stellar Amazon reviews. Place them on hold at the library. Tell your children about which books are coming down the pipeline and give them a little background to build anticipation. When the book arrives, sit together and read a few pages aloud to get them started.

Day 13

☐ Choose an activity to enjoy with your children for at least fifteen minutes. Books, sports, cooking, shopping, chores—your choice.

Your big job today is to create your long-term plan, which you will implement beginning on day 15.

By now you've had nearly two weeks to observe your children without any digital entertainment. It's possible that your detox was so successful that you want to continue on, completely screen-less. That's great! If you didn't promise your kids it would only last two weeks, then extending your detox should be simple. For very young kids, it is very easy to extend a detox. For older kids, this becomes a little trickier since a lot of kids' social lives and schoolwork today is facilitated online.

Next, using your journal, create your long-term plan. It should be individually tailored to your family and children. Turn back to chapters 7 and 8 for more help with creating a long-term plan. Welcome your older kids' feedback on the detox as you're formulating the plan. See the "Worksheet for Tweens and Teens" in the back of the book for help with that.

Day 14

☐ Congratulations, your family just completed an entire fourteen-day digital detox! Addiction experts have said that it can be more difficult to break tech habits than drug habits. You've gone against the cultural grain, and in doing so have achieved no small feat. Celebrate your detox with a fun outing or special meal. Share your observations with your kids. Ask them to tell you a few observations. If you haven't already, share your family's new long-term plan.

Worksheet for
Tweens and Teens

Your parents want you to be able to enjoy the great parts of your phone/computer in a healthy way. We know you want that too. What are some of your favorite ways to use technology?

_____

_____

_____

_____

_____

Each day has twenty-four hours. On the next page, fill in how much time you already spend doing each activity every day. Round up to the half hour, as time gets lost in transitioning activities.

Activity	Time
Sleeping	
School (including travel time)	
Homework	
Chores	
Work	
Meals	
Practicing sports	
Playing an instrument	
Exercising	
Hanging out with family (in person)	
Hanging out with friends (in person)	
Total	
Subtract the total from 24	

That's how much time is left in your day for everything else, including entertainment technology.

What proportion of that time do you think is reasonable and wise to allocate to consuming digital media entertainment, playing video games, or scrolling social media? (Remember, your free time is like a bank account balance. The more you spend on a screen, the less you have for everything else—hanging out with friends in real life, spending time with Mom and Dad, exercising, hiking, enjoying a family movie, playing a board game, baking, reading, practicing piano, down time.)

Creating Preventative Solutions

MODERN PARENTS often rely on digital diversions for the most tedious parts of the day: long commutes, periods of waiting, preventing boredom. When you suddenly remove that crutch, these daily scenarios can now bring additional stress. But with a little planning, that doesn't have to be the case. Here are some ideas to get you started. In your detox journal, write out some typical times your children would use a screen and name a feasible nonscreen activity your children might enjoy instead.

	Screen-free activity
Doctor appointment	Mad Libs
Bus stop	Play I Spy
Breakfast	Talk about upcoming stressors/goals/exciting parts of the day
Long commute	Notebook and washable coloring supplies
Working from home	A length of butcher paper and markers
Sibling's piano practice	Matchbox cars (for younger kids) or logic puzzle book (for older kids)
Grocery shopping	Letter-hunt game. Challenge younger kids to find the letters of the alphabet around the store. Assign older kids items on your list to find, and time them, *Supermarket Sweep*–style.
FOMO with classmates and online games	Invite one or two friends to come over and hang out in person. Plan an activity, take them to get smoothies, visit the driving range, go to the batting cages.

FAQs

When is the best time to begin?

A long weekend or extended vacation is ideal, or whenever both parents can be home. One fun option is to kick off a detox with a camping trip, where no internet reception is available.

That said, there is no perfect time to begin. So if you can't start on a weekend or the idea of camping makes you want to cry, just get your spouse on board and then pick a date on your calendar. Any day that ends in *y* will do.

I'm not really an organized person. I don't prep all my meals for the week on Sundays, my closets look like a shaken snow globe, and overscheduling makes my skin crawl. Are we still candidates for a detox?

Not only are you detox candidates, but we are also kindred spirits. I happen to enjoy living life by the seat of my pants. Give me some broad principles and let me live the day as it comes. If you are this way, you can absolutely detox—and with wonderful results.

I do recommend having several ideas ready for when things get wild. (Screamers in a store, fighting in the car at the drive-up pharmacy, etc.) Have your stacks of library books, your mental ideas for screen-free fun, and plenty of conversations with your spouse about observations and ideas. You do not have to check every box in this book for your detox to be effective. You do need to stick to its principles.

We are three days in and my life is harder than ever. Help!

Stay the course! Remember, different families hit their strides at different times. Some families enjoy great results immediately. Some take two weeks for things to finally click. Just like potty training!

At the end of the day, sit down and talk with your spouse about how and when things went wrong. Brainstorm preventative solutions for the next day. If necessary, you may need to implement consequences for terrible behaviors or tantrums related to a screen not being allowed. An additional chore? A treat being taken away? You could say that every tantrum adds an additional day to the detox. Do what you gotta do, Mom and Dad. But if you told your kids that the detox would last two weeks, and it hasn't been two weeks, DO. NOT. CAVE.

We have found most often that when spit really hits the fan in parenting, one-on-one time with a parent and child is the most effective relational bridge. Plop on the couch and chat. Go for a walk. A drive. Fill their love tanks. Fill it in the morning, and throughout the day as often as you can. Eye contact, back-and-forth conversation, hugs, giggles. Take ten minutes to play checkers or Go Fish. These intentional moments are so much more consequential than loading the dishwasher, even though the dishes feel more urgent. If these windows of time don't already exist in your day, make them.

Okay, I know you said not to quit before two weeks, but two days in my kids were screaming and I had to take a work call, so I handed over the iPads. What do I do now?

I recommend huddling with your spouse to make your initial detox plan more fail-proof. Take what you've learned and try again. One mama was in the same boat and knew she was more likely to cave again when the going got tough. Before they began their second attempt, she asked her husband to hide the kids' tablets and not tell her where. This way, she couldn't cave even if she wanted to. Their second attempt at a detox was a resounding success.

If your kids are at a neighbor's or friend's house, and the adult in charge allows for screen time unknowingly, no sweat. Move forward. But if your kids sneak screen time, or if you as the parent break your own detox on day four, you will be undermining yourself. At that point, I recommend starting over. Show your kids what it looks like to make a plan and stick to it. If that means you have to begin again, that's okay. Take a breath and explain to the kids that your fourteen-day counter will start over. Your commitment to keeping your word will diminish their incentive to sneak screen time or hound you about using screen time before the end of the detox.

I'm concerned my child has a deeper problem than can be solved by our detox. The aggression/depression/anxiety alarms us in ways that our detox alone is not solving. Help.

Not every problem is caused by a screen. And if your family is struggling with a behavioral, psychiatric, or medical issue, by all means contact a professional medical doctor, counselor, psychiatrist, or any expert you deem appropriate for your situation. I am not a medical doctor, and while the advice in this book has been tried and tested on many families, that doesn't preclude the existence of a medical or chemical problem. If you do observe that your child's episodes are worse with screen use, be sure to relay this information to any professional help you do seek.

I noticed this book is tailored for families with kids fourteen and under. What if my child is older than that and needs a detox. Any advice?

Great question. Older kids can absolutely benefit from a detox. It's much simpler to declare a rule change for younger kids, because parents naturally have more of an authority role when kids are small. As children grow older, our parental role begins to slowly switch from authority to half-authority, half-mentor. By the time our kids move out of the house, our role of authority will have tapered off completely. That's by design, and it's good.

Detoxing kids in that middle zone is going to look different from detoxing young kids.

Here are tips for a detox for kids older than fourteen:

Tell your kids about all the research and benefits of a detox. Ask if they've ever felt ignored or disconnected from their friends, or even you (gulp!), because of a device. Ask if they've ever felt anxious or depressed after being on their device for a while. Share how you've felt the same way.

Share why you've decided to take this on, despite momentary sacrifice. "We want a fresh start for how we use tech in our home, so we are going to take a two-week break, and then bring back in only the specific parts of technology that we actually want. I know it feels scary and stressful to take on a challenge like this, especially considering how much of our lives are spent on devices. But the research is compelling. A break from tech can really help your mental health!"

Implementing a detox for your youngest kids doesn't necessarily require a parent to detox themselves, but a detox with teens is a different story. It is wise to choose some aspect of your own tech use to detox alongside your kids. Social media? Netflix? Get in the detox with them. Share your own goals, what you hope to get out of these two weeks.

Cold turkey might need some qualifiers for teens. Maybe you will keep your child's phone for two weeks. Maybe that's not feasible due to carpool situations. An increasing amount of schoolwork is completed online. You will need to get into the weeds on a specific detox plan for older kids. If your child says, "But I need my phone for X assignment," then maybe you will allow phones in common areas, and delete all apps except those necessary for school. Set parental controls so that no apps may be downloaded.

Your teen's detox plan will need to be individually tailored. That said, even a professional teenage influencer or YouTuber could take a two-week break from the computer without the world ending. Social media, video games, YouTube—all digital entertainment can easily be removed for two weeks without incident.

You will want to use some of the principles throughout the book, along with the principles found in chapter 12, "Tech for Mom and Dad," as you design your teenager's detox.

Ask if any of your kids' friends are willing to detox with them. One high school teacher told me that a majority of her class said they wished they lived in a time when smartphones didn't exist. Yet these kids won't willingly take a break because no one is requiring them to do so. And no kid wants to be the odd one out. But if a cluster of friends decides together to take a two-week break, soon they're making their own collective lists, hanging out after school in person, jogging together. There is strength in numbers.

- Ask your kids to share what they want their tech use to look like.
- Ask them if they've observed other people using devices in a way that annoyed them or made them feel unseen.
- Ask them how much of their days they'd like to look back on and see was spent being entertained.
- Ask them if they ever feel in a funk after a lot of screen time.

Tell them your own honest answers to these questions, and share that you're just trying to get this right for both of you. It's only two weeks, and you will make your own long-term plans together at the end of this thing. Give them some ownership by allowing them to choose some facets like start date, a specific family outing to happen during the detox, the first family movie to be watched at the end of the detox, dinner on the first night of the detox, specific days to have friends come over during the detox, etc.

Recommended Reading

Parenting Distraction

Christakis, Erika. "The Dangers of Distracted Parenting." *Atlantic*, July/August 2018. https://www.theatlantic.com/magazine/archive/2018/07/the-dangers-of-distracted-parenting/561752/.

Fallows, James. "The Art of Staying Focused in a Distracting World." *Atlantic*, June 2013. https://www.theatlantic.com/magazine/archive/2013/06/the-art-of-paying-attention/309312/.

Reinke, Tony. *12 Ways Your Phone Is Changing You*. Wheaton, IL: Crossway, 2017.

Newport, Cal. *Digital Minimalism: Choosing a Focused Life in a Noisy World*. New York: Penguin/Portfolio, 2019.

Sax, Leonard. *The Collapse of Parenting: How We Hurt Our Kids When We Treat Them Like Grown-Ups*. New York: Basic, 2017.

Stone, Linda. "Beyond Simple Multi-Tasking: Continuous Partial Attention." Linda Stone (blog), November 30, 2009. https://lindastone.net/2009/11/30/beyond-simple-multi-tasking-continuous-partial-attention/.

Reading Aloud

Mackenzie, Sarah. *The Read-Aloud Family: Making Meaningful and Lasting Connections with Your Kids*. Grand Rapids, MI: Zondervan, 2018.

Mackenzie also hosts a delightful podcast where she interviews authors and all kinds of guests. She's a mother of six, and her website is home to the gold standard of booklists for every interest and age.

Prior, Karen Swallow. *On Reading Well: Finding the Good Life through Great Books*. Grand Rapids, MI: Brazos, 2018.

Prior is a beautiful writer and English professor. She addresses specific virtues in each chapter (like prudence, temperance, humility, and patience), explaining why each is necessary for human flourishing and civil society. She encourages readers to learn to love life, literature, and God through reading well. The book is not specifically geared toward parents or children, but I found it foundationally motivating.

Trelease, Jim. *Jim Trelease's Read-Aloud Handbook*. 8th ed. Edited and revised by Cyndi Giorgis. New York: Penguin, 2019.

No wonder this book has eight editions and has sold more than a million copies. The first half of this book answers the why and how of reading aloud. Try reading and not feeling compelled to fill your home with books. The second half is a treasury of recommended read-aloud books. This is a good one to own and mark up with all your notes.

Smartphones and Porn

Jenson, Kristen A. *Good Pictures Bad Pictures: Porn-Proofing Today's Young Kids*. 2nd ed. Kennewick, WA: Glen Cove Press, 2018.

Tech and Older Kids

Crouch, Amy. *My Tech-Wise Life: Growing Up and Making Choices in a World of Devices*. Grand Rapids, MI: Baker Books, 2020.

Crouch, Andy. *The Tech-Wise Family: Everyday Steps for Putting Technology in Its Proper Place*. Grand Rapids, MI: Baker Books, 2017.

McKee, Jonathan. *The Teen's Guide to Social Media and Mobile Devices: 21 Tips to Wise Posting in an Insecure World*. Uhrichsville, OH: Shiloh Run, 2017.

Sales, Nancy Jo. *American Girls: Social Media and the Secret Lives of Teenagers*. New York: Penguin, 2016.

Hazards of the Digital World, Electronic Screen Syndrome

Dunckley, Victoria. *Reset Your Child's Brain: A Four-Week Plan to End Meltdowns, Raise Grades, and Boost Social Skills by Reversing the Effects of Electronic Screen-Time.* Novato, CA: New World Library, 2015.

Kardaras, Nicholas. *Glow Kids: How Screen Addiction Is Hijacking Our Kids—and How to Break the Trance.* New York: St. Martin's Press, 2016.

Acknowledgments

FIRST, I want to give a huge high-five to all the parents who have made the decision to do the hard, counter-cultural thing and implement a digital detox. Telling your kids that they're taking a screen break is like jumping off a cliff. I hope this book has felt like a parachute. I believe you've been divinely chosen to shepherd, love, and direct your child, and I'm honored that you've let me share in a small part of that.

I can't overstate my gratitude for my husband, David—proofreader, editor, organizer, child-feeder, encourager, cool-headed leader, car DJ, lightsaber instructor, talk-me-off-the-cliff-er, and breadwinner. Without you, there'd be no book. (And no kids, for that matter.) Thanks for everything. You are the salt to my fries.

Selah, Jack, Carter, Caroline, Elaina, and every child who has come and gone in our home (whose real names I've changed in the book and withheld here for privacy)—you kids are the most beautiful gifts of my life, and I am so grateful that God gave me you. Thanks for letting me detox you. Thanks for thanking me for detoxing you. Your giggles, giant saucer eyes, deep theological questions, and hilarious jokes feed my heart and soul. What a privilege it is to mother you.

To my agent, Cynthia Ruchti, your perspective as an author and agent has been tremendously helpful on this journey. Your advocacy skills and editor's eye are a gift. (Is there anything you can't do?!) Your faith and encouragement are continually appreciated. You are a gem.

To my editor, Jennifer Dukes Lee, I knew this book was in good hands with you. Your faith, talent, and kindness made me feel less like I was giving away my book baby and more like I was sending her to finishing school at her loving aunt's farm where cute baby pigs arrive on school buses.

To Mark Rice and Deirdre Close, your expertise has blessed me so much. Your team is second to none. I knew after that first Zoom call that this match was a good one, but you guys kept raising the bar. Stop! Stop raising the bar, it's too high!

To Brooke Martinez, thank you for your coaching, help, and advice. Angela Bouma, you are talented in arenas that I don't even come close to grasping. Thank you for everything.

To the moms and dads who agreed to let me help them detox their kids and share their stories in this book: Marissa and Jarod, Kim and Ben, Sharon and Luke, Erika and Carlos, Candice and Dan, Ashley and Justin, Megan and John, Caitlin and Mark, Emily and Darren, Tacie and John, Tina and Casey, and those who wish to remain anonymous. I am so encouraged by you all.

To the friends, teens, teachers, doctors, and experts who let me pick their brains about parenting and screen time: Jen, Peyton, and Kendall; Lauren, George Petersen, Dr. Leonard Sax, Monica Gomez, Matt Miles, Joe Clement.

To the authors, researchers, and experts whose work has blown my mind and affirmed our experiences on this journey: Sherry Turkle, Victoria Dunckley, Nicholas Kardaras, Andy Crouch, Jean Twenge, Sarah Mackenzie, Tony Reinke, Daniel Siegel, Tina Payne Bryson, Dana Suskind, Catherine Steiner-Adair, Richard Freed, Clay and Sally Clarkson, Arlene Pellicane, Neil Postman, Jim Trelease, Cyndi Giorgis. Thank you for your work in this field!

To Pattie, my mentor and friend. Thank you for speaking life and encouragement into my overthinking brain. You are always pointing me to Jesus, and I am eternally grateful.

To Dasha and Mom D., thank you for caring for our kids while I wrote this book. We appreciate you so much.

To my sister Ashley, whose encouragement, wisdom, editing, and gut checks have helped me countless times. I treasure your friendship most of all.

To my mom, for staying home to raise me, for teaching childhood me the comfort of a calm and loving parent.

And to my dad, Dennis Snee. My hero, my favorite writer. The kindest, gentlest, funniest, and coolest person I've known. You showed me the power of a present and attentive dad. M/D Club forever. I miss you every day.

Notes

Introduction

1. This digital detox is designed for and has been tested by families with children from infancy through age fourteen. The foundational principles still work for people older than that, although modifications will be necessary. See chapter 12 for examples of adult detoxes, and the FAQs section at the end for tips on digitally detoxing kids older than fourteen.

Chapter 1 Parenting Challenges for a New Generation—The Problem

1. Andy Crouch, *The Tech-Wise Family: Everyday Steps for Putting Technology in Its Proper Place* (Grand Rapids, MI: Baker Books, 2017), 22–23.

2. Selim Algar, "Screen Time for Kids Explodes During Coronavirus Crisis, Study Says," *New York Post*, April 23, 2020, https://nypost.com/2020/04/23/screen-time-for-kids-explodes-during-coronavirus-crisis-study/.

3. Victoria Dunckley, *Reset Your Child's Brain: A Four-Week Plan to End Meltdowns, Raise Grades, and Boost Social Skills by Reversing the Effects of Electronic Screen-Time* (Novato, CA: New World Library, 2015), 57.

4. Norihito Oshima et al., "The Suicidal Feelings, Self-Injury, and Mobile Phone Use after Lights Out in Adolescents," *Journal of Pediatric Psychology*, 37, no. 9 (October 2012), 1023–1030.

5. Oshima et al., 1023–1030.

6. Quoted in "Screen Dependency Disorder: The Effects of 'Screen Time' Addiction," Neurohealth Associates, February 11, 2020, https://nhahealth.com/screen-dependency-disorder-the-effects-of-screen-time-addiction/.

7. Victoria Rideout and Michael B. Robb, *The Common Sense Census: Media Use by Kids Age Zero to Eight, 2020* (San Francisco: Common Sense Media), 4, https://www.commonsensemedia.org/sites/default/files/uploads/research/2020_zero_to_eight_census_final_web.pdf.

8. Rideout and Robb, *Media Use by Kids*, 3.

9. Jason Nagata et al., "Screen Time Use among US Adolescents During the COVID-19 Pandemic: Findings from the Adolescent Brain Cognitive Development

(ABCD) Study," *JAMA Pediatrics*, November 1, 2021, https://jamanetwork.com
/journals/jamapediatrics/fullarticle/2785686.

10. Vicky Rideout, *Common Sense Census: Media Use by Tweens and Teens,
2015* (San Francisco: Common Sense Media), 13, https://www.commonsensemedia
.org/sites/default/files/uploads/research/census_researchreport.pdf.

11. Maryanne Wolf, *Reader, Come Home: The Reading Brain in a Digital
World* (New York: Harper, 2018), 110.

12. Gadi Lissak, "Adverse Physiological and Psychological Effects of Screen Time
on Children and Adolescents: Literature Review and Case Study," *Environmental Research* 164, no. 1 (July 2018): 149–157, https://doi.org/10.1016/j.envres.2018.01.015.

13. Michelle Pine, "Screentime and Toddlers, with Occupational Therapist,"
The Collin Kartchner Podcast, August 28, 2020, 12:30.

14. Donna Hermawati et al., "Early Electronic Screen Exposure and Autistic-
Like Symptoms," *Intractable & Rare Diseases Research* 7, no. 1 (February 19,
2018): 69–71, https://dx.doi.org/10.5582/irdr.2018.01007.

15. Dunckley, *Reset Your Child's Brain*, 17.

16. George Petersen, email message to author, February 2, 2021.

17. Martin Korte, "The Impact of the Digital Revolution on Human Brain
and Behavior: Where Do We Stand?," *Dialogues in Clinical Neuroscience* 22, no.
2 (June 2020): 101–111, https://dx.doi.org/10.31887/DCNS.2020.22.2/mkorte.

18. Sherry Turkle, *Reclaiming Conversation: The Power of Talk in a Digital
Age* (New York: Penguin, 2015), 28.

Chapter 2 Unplug Cold Turkey

1. Turkle, *Reclaiming Conversation*, 322.

2. Marie Evans Schmidt et al., "The Effects of Background Television on
the Toy Play Behavior of Very Young Children," *Child Development*, 79, no. 4
(2008): 1137–51.

3. Turkle, *Reclaiming Conversation*, 213.

Chapter 3 Notice Your Kids' Interests, Talents, Opportunities for Growth

1. Derek Kidner, *Proverbs: An Introduction and Commentary* (Downers Grove,
IL: IVP Academic, 2009), 139.

2. Kip and Mona Lisa Harding, *The Brainy Bunch: The Harding Family's
Method to College Ready by Age Twelve* (New York: Gallery, 2014), 22.

3. Josh Shipp, "Your Child's Most Annoying Trait May Just Reveal Their Greatest Strengths," TEDx Talks, October 18, 2017, https://youtu.be/mU5WO93Kw4E.

Chapter 4 Develop a List of Screen-Free Fun Together

1. Nicholas Kardaras, *Glow Kids: How Screen Addiction Is Hijacking Our
Kids—and How to Break the Trance* (New York: St. Martin's Press, 2016), 124.

2. Crouch, *Tech-Wise Family*, 139.

3. Gabe and Rebekah Lyons, "Two Callings under One Roof," keynote speech,
EDGE|X 2020, October 2, 2020, https://www.edgementoring.org/gabe-rebekah
-lyons.

Chapter 5 Open the Books!

1. *Jim Trelease's Read-Aloud Handbook*, 8th ed., ed. and rev. Cyndi Giorgis (New York: Penguin, 2019), 4.

2. *Jim Trelease's Read-Aloud Handbook* (2019), 69.

3. *Jim Trelease's Read-Aloud Handbook* (2019), 69.

4. *Jim Trelease's Read-Aloud Handbook* (2019), 69.

5. Sarah Knutson, "Statistics on the Scores of Middle School Students Who Read," Classroom (website), September 26, 2017, https://classroom.synonym.com/statistics-scores-middle-school-students-read-15916.html.

6. Timothy A. Keller and Marcel Adam Just, "Altering Cortical Connectivity: Remediation-Induced Changes in the White Matter of Poor Readers," *Neuron* 64, no. 5 (2009): 624–31, https://doi.org/10.1016/j.neuron.2009.10.018.

7. Sarah Mackenzie, "Books for Teens, and Why YA Is a Genre (Not a Reading Level)," July 8, 2019, in *Read-Aloud Revival*, podcast, 32:52, https://readaloudrevival.com/132.

Chapter 6 Reading Aloud: The Magic Ticket

1. Anna E. Duursma, "The Effects of Fathers' and Mothers' Reading to Their Children on Language Outcomes of Children Participating in Early Head Start in the United States," *Fathering: a Journal of Theory and Research about Men as Parents*, 12, no. 3 (2014): 283–302, https://ro.uow.edu.au/cgi/viewcontent.cgi?article=2345&context=sspapers.

2. Janelle M. Gray, "Reading Achievement and Autonomy as a Function of Father-to-Son Reading" (master's thesis, California State University, 1991).

3. *Jim Trelease's Read-Aloud Handbook* (2019), 87–98.

4. Mem Fox, *Reading Magic: Why Reading Aloud to Our Children Will Change Their Lives Forever*, upd. and rev. ed. (Orlando: Harcourt, 2008), 17.

5. Jim Trelease, *The Read-Aloud Handbook*, 7th ed., (New York: Penguin, 2013), 19–20.

6. Mackenzie, *Read-Aloud Family*, 27.

7. Dana Suskind, *Thirty Million Words: Building a Child's Brain* (New York: Dutton, 2015), 22.

8. Trelease, *The Read-Aloud Handbook* (2013), 41.

9. Suskind, *Thirty Million Words*, 73.

Chapter 7 Creating a Long-Term Plan for Younger Kids

1. Gary Chapman and Arlene Pellicane, *Growing Up Social: Raising Relational Kids in a Screen-Driven World* (Chicago: Northfield, 2014), 124.

2. Jonathan McKee, *The Teen's Guide to Social Media and Mobile Devices: 21 Tips to Wise Posting in an Insecure World* (Uhrichsville, OH: Shiloh Run, 2017), 11.

3. Chapman and Pellicane, *Growing Up Social*, 107.

4. Turkle, *Reclaiming Conversation*.

5. Crouch, *Tech-Wise Family*, 108.

6. "Frequently Asked Questions," Wait Until 8th, accessed October 25, 2021, https://www.waituntil8th.org/faqs.

7. Collin Kartchner, "Whatever age you're OK with them to start looking at porn," Instagram highlight, September 27, 2020, https://www.instagram.com /stories/highlights/18123720223136355/.

8. "The Crisis," Culture Reframed, accessed October 25, 2021, https://www .culturereframed.org/the-porn-crisis/.

Chapter 8 Creating a Long-Term Plan for Older Kids

1. Leonard Sax, *The Collapse of Parenting: How We Hurt Our Kids When We Treat Them Like Grown-Ups* (New York: Basic, 2017).

2. Gordon Neufeld and Gabor Maté, *Hold On to Your Kids: Why Parents Need to Matter More Than Peers*, upd. ed. (New York: Ballantine Books, 2014), 7.

3. Robert B. Cialdini, *Influence: The Psychology of Persuasion*, new and exp. ed. (New York: Harper Business, 2021), 114.

4. Jean M. Twenge, *iGen: Why Today's Super-Connected Kids Are Growing Up Less Rebellious, More Tolerant, Less Happy—and Completely Unprepared for Adulthood—and What That Means for the Rest of Us* (New York: Atria, 2018), 77–78.

5. Twenge, *iGen*, 74.

6. Twenge, *iGen*, 291–292.

7. "Understanding the Teen's Brain," Stanford Children's Health, accessed November 30, 2021, https://www.stanfordchildrens.org/en/topic/default?id=under standing-the-teen-brain-1-3051.

Chapter 9 Great Uses for Screens: Tech and Leisure

1. Twenge, *iGen*, 71–72.

2. Brooke Auxier et al., "Parenting Children in the Age of Screens," Pew Research Center, July 28, 2020, https://www.pewresearch.org/internet/2020/07 /28/parenting-children-in-the-age-of-screens/.

3. Auxier, "Parenting Children in the Age of Screens."

4. Lisa Rapaport, "Parents Think Teens Spend Too Much Time Playing Video Games," Reuters, January 20, 2020, https://www.reuters.com/article/us-health -teens-gaming/parents-think-teens-spend-too-much-time-playing-video-games -idUSKBN1ZJ25M.

5. Turkle, *Reclaiming Conversation*, 7.

6. Hope M. Cummings and Elizabeth A. Vandewater, "Relation of Adolescent Video Game Play to Time Spent in Other Activities," *Archives of Pediatric & Adolescent Medicine*, 161, no. 7 (July 2007): 684–689, https://doi.org/10.1001 /archpedi.161.7.684.

7. Chad Sapieha, "Grand Theft Auto V Game Review," Common Sense Media, https://www.commonsensemedia.org/game-reviews/grand-theft-auto-v.

8. Shaunti Feldhahn, "2 Things to Do If You Want Your Teen to Talk to You," Shaunti Feldhahn (website), June 29, 2016, https://shaunti.com/2016/06/2-things -to-do-if-you-want-your-teen-to-talk-to-you/.

9. Nancy Jo Sales, *American Girls: Social Media and the Secret Lives of Teenagers*, (New York: Penguin, 2016), 18.

10. Task Force on the Sexualization of Girls, *Report of the APA Task Force on the Sexualization of Girls, 2007* (Washington, DC: American Psychological Association), 21, http://www.apa.org/pi/women/programs/girls/report-full.pdf.

11. U.S. Department of Education National Center for Education Statistics, *Adult Literacy in the United States*, July 2019, https://nces.ed.gov/pubs2019/2019179/index.asp.

12. Michael Pollan, "Unhappy Meals," *New York Times Magazine*, January 28, 2007, https://www.nytimes.com/2007/01/28/magazine/28nutritionism.t.html.

Chapter 10 Tech and Learning

1. Tim Carmody, "'What's Wrong With Education Cannot Be Fixed with Technology'—The Other Steve Jobs," *Wired*, January 17, 2012, https://www.wired.com/2012/01/apple-education-jobs/.

2. Quoted in Kardaras, *Glow Kids*, 31.

3. Turkle, *Reclaiming Conversation*, 225–226.

4. Victoria Prooday, "Why Are Our Children So Bored at School, Cannot Wait, Get Easily Frustrated and Have No Real Friends?," YourOT.com, May 2016, https://yourot.com/parenting-club/2016/5/16/why-our-children-are-so-bored-at-school-cant-wait-and-get-so-easily-frustrated.

5. Monica Gomez, in conversation with the author, [NEED DATE].

6. Jenny Radesky and Dimitri Christakis, "Media and Young Minds," *Pediatrics* 138, no. 5 (November 2016): e20162591, https://doi.org/10.1542/peds.2016-2591.

7. Sheri Madigan et al., "Association Between Screen Time and Children's Performance on a Developmental Screening Test," *JAMA Pediatrics* 173, no. 3 (January 28, 2019): 244–250, http://dx.doi.org/10.1001/jamapediatrics.2018.5056.

8. Catherine Steiner-Adair, *The Big Disconnect: Protecting Childhood and Family Relationships in the Digital Age* (New York: Harper, 2013), 80.

9. Joe Clement, in conversation with the author, February 18, 2021.

10. Twenge, *iGen*, 31, 33.

11. Matt Miles, in conversation with the author, February 18, 2021.

12. Clifford Nass, interviewed by Ira Flatow, "The Myth of Multitasking," *Talk of the Nation*, NPR, May 10, 2013, https://www.npr.org/2013/05/10/182861382/the-myth-of-multitasking.

13. Quoted in Kardaras, *Glow Kids*, 32.

14. Rideout, *Media Use by Tweens and Teens*, 16.

15. Quoted in Twenge, *iGen*, 188–190.

16. Wim Westera, "Games Are Motivating, Aren't They? Disputing the Arguments for Digital Game-Based Learning," *International Journal of Serious Games* 2, no. 2 (June 2015): 3–17, http://dx.doi.org/10.17083/ijsg.v2i2.58.

17. Westera, "Games Are Motivating, Aren't They?," 5.

18. Joe Clement and Matt Miles, *Screen Schooled: Two Veteran Teachers Expose How Technology Overuse Is Making Our Kids Dumber* (Chicago: Chicago Review Press, 2018), 35–36.

19. Quoted in Connie Huang, "Too Much Screen Time?," *University Child Development School* (blog), July 11, 2020, https://www.ucds.org/too-much-screen-time/.

20. Sandi Mann and Rebekah Cadman, "Does Being Bored Make Us More Creative?," *Creativity Research Journal* 26, no. 2 (May 8, 2014), 165–173, https://doi.org/10.1080/10400419.2014.901073.

21. Lauren [last name withheld], in conversation with the author, March 2021.

22. Nir Eyal, "Stanford Psychology Expert: This Is the No. 1 Skill Parents Need to Teach Their Kids—But Most Don't," CNBC, September 10, 2019, https://www.cnbc.com/2019/09/10/stanford-psychology-expert-biggest-parenting-mistake-is-not-teaching-kids-this-important-skill.html.

23. Leonard Sax, email message to author, February 9, 2021.

24. Petersen, email.

Chapter 11 A Detox and Long-Term Plan for Every Kind of Family

1. Twenge, *iGen*, 84.

2. Dunckley, *Reset Your Child's Brain*, 93.

Chapter 12 Tech for Mom and Dad

1. Jeffrey I. Cole et al., *Surveying the Digital Future: The 16th Annual Study on the Impact of Digital Technology on Americans* (Los Angeles: Center for the Digital Future at USC Annenberg, 2018), 87, https://www.digitalcenter.org/wp-content/uploads/2018/12/2018-Digital-Future-Report.pdf.

2. Noah Zandan, "Eye Contact—A Declining Communications Tool?," *Quantified Communications Blog*, accessed October 7, 2021, https://www.quantified.ai/blog/eye-contact-a-declining-communications-tool/.

3. Marie Haaland, "Parents Only Spend 24 More Minutes with Their Kids Than Their Phones," *New York Post*, October 21, 2019, https://nypost.com/2019/10/21/parents-only-spend-24-more-minutes-with-their-kids-than-their-phones/.

4. Ellen Rose, "Continuous Partial Attention: Reconsidering the Role of Online Learning in the Age of Interruption," *Educational Technology* 50, no. 4 (July–August 2010): 41–46, http://www.jstor.org/stable/44429840.

5. "Time Flies: U.S. Adults Now Spend Nearly Half a Day Interacting with Media," Nielsen Insights, July 31, 2018, https://www.nielsen.com/us/en/insights/article/2018/time-flies-us-adults-now-spend-nearly-half-a-day-interacting-with-media/.

6. Haaland, "Parents Only Spend 24 More Minutes with Their Kids Than Their Phones."

7. Crouch, *Tech-Wise Family*, 104.

8. Haaland, "Parents Only Spend 24 More Minutes with Their Kids Than Their Phones."

9. Colleen Cordes and Edward Miller, eds., *Fool's Gold: A Critical Look at Computers in Childhood* (College Park, MD: Alliance for Childhood, 2000), 28.

10. Gomez, conversation.

11. Clement and Miles, *Screen Schooled*, 81.

12. Turkle, *Reclaiming Conversation*, 213.

13. Quoted in Clement and Miles, *Screen Schooled*, 142.

14. Steiner-Adair, *The Big Disconnect*, 269.

15. Daniel J. Siegel and Tina Payne Bryson, *The Whole-Brain Child: 12 Revolutionary Strategies to Nurture Your Child's Developing Mind* (New York: Bantam, 2012), 7.

Molly DeFrank is a stay-at-home mom and foster mom to many. She graduated with a degree in international relations from the University of California, Davis. Molly married her college sweetheart and a week later began working for an actor-turned-Governator.

After a few years, she put that life on hold to raise several amazing tiny people. She assumed stay-at-home mom life would prove easier than the fast pace and stress of the working world. Nope. But she wouldn't trade the time spent loving and pouring into her precious humans for anything.

Molly is passionate about loving God and loving people, and teaching her kids to do the same. She longs to encourage moms with gospel hope and peace amid the chaotic and stressful days of motherhood.

Molly enjoys time spent across a table with friends, reading instead of cleaning, and black coffee strong enough to power a small jet. She's also a recovering vegetarian. Send help, send tofu, drop her a line on Facebook or Instagram or on her website, www.mollydefrank.com.